Appetizers
and
Small Meals

Most HPBooks are available at special quantity discounts for bulk purchases for sales promotions, premiums, fund-raising or educational use. Special books, or book excerpts, can also be created to fit specific needs.

For details, write: Special Markets, The Berkley Publishing Group, 200 Madison Avenue, New York, New York 10016.

Appetizers
and
Small Meals

Mable Hoffman

HPBooks

HPBooks
Published by The Berkley Publishing Group
A member of Penguin Putnam Inc.
200 Madison Avenue
New York, NY 10016

Copyright © 1997 by Mable Hoffman
Book design by Paula R. Szafranski
Cover design by Joe Lanni
Cover photograph copyright © by FoodPix

All rights reserved. This book, or parts thereof,
may not be reproduced in any form without permission.

First edition: December 1997

Published simultaneously in Canada.

The Putnam Berkley World Wide Web site address is http://www.berkley.com

Library of Congress Cataloging-in-Publication Data

Hoffman, Mable.
    Appetizers and small meals / Mable Hoffman. — 1st ed.
      p. cm.
    Includes index.
    ISBN 1-55788-277-0
    1. Appetizers. I. Title.
TX740.H6153 1997
641.8'12—dc21   97-861
                                                                     CIP

Notice: The information printed in this book is true and complete to the best of our knowledge. All recommendations are made without any guarantees on the part of the author or the publisher. The author and publisher disclaim all liability in connection with the use of this information.

Printed in the United States of America

10 9 8 7 6 5 4 3 2 1

Contents

Acknowledgments	vii
Introduction	ix
Little Savory Bites	1
Small Meals	71
All Wrapped Up	105
Salads	123
Breads and Sandwiches	143
Dips, Spreads and Pâtés	187
Microwaved Appetizers and Small Meals	225
Metric Conversion Charts	241
Index	242

Acknowledgments

Special thanks to Jan Robertson for her invaluable assistance. Thanks to Grace Wheeler for recipe testing and to Mike Robertson for doing all the word processing for the book.

Introduction

Changing Trends

Today, our eating habits are changing. The traditional custom of breakfast, lunch and dinner is often bypassed because of our busy and unpredictable lifestyles. In the past, most of us thought of appetizers as foods to be consumed before the main part of our evening meal or at parties. Within the past several years, we have realized that our favorite appetizers may be grouped together as a delicious substitute for heavier main dishes.

Even the typical time-consuming miniature hors d'oeuvres are often replaced with more practical finger foods. If necessary, today's hostess or host will add one or more hearty dishes to satisfy hungry guests. This trend is a reflection of menus from many of the most popular restaurants in our country. Often replacing a multi-course menu starting with appetizers and ending with desserts is a wide choice of mini-courses for you to put together to suit your tastes.

Family food is being influenced by today's variety of lifestyles. With various family members on different schedules, a different kind of dinner is evolving. Those eating a hearty business lunch are not ready for a heavy dinner. Also, those with evening classes or appointments do not have time for the traditional old-fashioned sit-down dinner. This book is designed for all those families whose members have a variety of demanding schedules, as well as for today's home entertaining.

Fortunately, our supermarkets and food specialty stores support these trends with innovative merchandising techniques. They offer new sizes and shapes of many popular products. For example, the variety of regular and boneless poultry parts offers many opportunities to experiment. The emphasis on fresh seasonal vegetables and fruits from various parts of the world makes it easier for us to include these items in our appetizers and small meals. The inclusion of popular combinations of dried beans, rice or pasta with small amounts of fish, poultry or cheese will inspire many ideas for intriguing small meals as well as appetizers. Many of these recipes will provide you with a welcome contribution to your next pot-luck get-together.

Choosing an Appetizer or Small-Meal Menu

There is a wide range of choices for this type of menu. There are no rigid rules to follow. If you are serving appetizers before a hearty dinner, it is wise to choose two or three fairly light recipes. A heartier selection often encourages guests to fill up on appetizers, spoiling their enjoyment of your dinner.

It is difficult to select a specific kind of appetizer that appeals to all of your guests. That's why it is better to make small quantities of several recipes rather than one large batch of your favorite one. Most people enjoy tasting small amounts even though they might not like it enough to ask for your recipe.

Try to select appetizers that can be made ahead of time. Make them the day before and refrigerate. Or, even better, choose one or more that can be frozen. Prepare them a week or two before the party and keep them in the freezer until the day before they're needed.

Serving the Food

For many people, the most important factor is to serve hot food *hot* and cold food *cold*. To do this, watch the clock and be prepared to take hot food out of the oven or the pot just in time to serve your guests. Also, it is handy to use slow cookers, chafing dishes or hot trays. This assures you that the last guest will enjoy the same hot food as the first person in the buffet line. The microwave oven can also be helpful in warming made-ahead dishes just before serving.

Remember that interesting colors and textures are impressive when food is arranged on platters or trays. If the basic food is not colorful, garnish the plates with contrasting foods such as cherry tomatoes, orange slices, red apple wedges, small clusters of grapes and strips of red, green or yellow peppers.

Little Savory Bites

Serve the following dishes as part of a menu for a party, as a snack or even a complete meal, using a selection of appetizers containing chicken, meat, seafood and vegetables. Offering foods in small pieces allows guests to try several dishes and choose their favorites.

If serving a selection of dishes, choose flavors that are compatible, and think about color, texture and temperature as well. Garnish platters with colorful accents that can be eaten with the appetizers.

Chicken Barrel Roll-Ups

A package of thin uncooked turkey cutlets makes a good substitute for chicken.

1 to 1 1/4 pounds boneless, skinless chicken breasts
1 cup ground cooked ham
2 cups soft bread crumbs
4 ounces (1 cup) Cheddar cheese, shredded
1 tablespoon finely chopped green onion
1 teaspoon prepared mustard
1 egg, slightly beaten

Tarragon-Butter Sauce

1/3 cup margarine or butter, melted
1 tablespoon white-wine vinegar
1 tablespoon fresh lemon juice
1 tablespoon finely chopped fresh tarragon or 1 teaspoon dried tarragon
1/4 teaspoon salt
1/8 teaspoon pepper

Partially freeze chicken to make it easier to slice. Lightly pound chicken with a meat mallet to an even thickness. With a sharp knife, cut lengthwise into 28 to 30 thin slices; set aside.

Combine ham, bread crumbs, cheese, green onion, mustard and egg in a medium bowl. Form 1 tablespoon of bread mixture into a barrel shape about 1 1/4 inches long. Wrap in a strip of chicken breast. Repeat until all of mixture and chicken are used. Thread 3 or 4 rolls on 10- to 12-inch metal skewers.

Prepare sauce.

Preheat grill or broiler. Brush kabobs with sauce. Grill or broil 4 to 5 inches from heat source 5 minutes. Brush with sauce; turn kabobs. Cook another 4 to 5 minutes or until chicken is no longer pink and filling is set.

Makes 28 to 30 roll-ups.

Tarragon-Butter Sauce

Combine all sauce ingredients in a small bowl; stir to combine.

Bombay Chicken Pinwheels

When making the Dipping Sauce, be sure to finely chop all pieces of fruit in the chutney.

4 boneless, skinless chicken-breast halves (about 1 pound)
1 tablespoon Dijon mustard
1 tablespoon margarine or butter, melted
1/4 teaspoon salt
1/8 teaspoon pepper
2 tablespoons margarine or butter

DIPPING SAUCE

1/4 cup chutney, fruit finely chopped
1/2 cup peanut butter
1/2 cup chicken broth or bouillon
1 tablespoon honey
1/4 teaspoon crushed red pepper flakes
1 clove garlic, crushed

Lightly pound chicken breasts between 2 sheets of waxed paper until about 1/4 inch thick. Combine mustard, 1 tablespoon melted margarine or butter, salt and pepper in a small bowl. Spread top side of pounded chicken pieces with mustard mixture. Starting with long edge, tightly roll chicken like a jelly roll. Secure with a small wooden pick. Repeat with remaining chicken.

In a 10-inch skillet, melt 2 tablespoons margarine or butter. Add chicken rolls; cook over medium-low heat about 10 minutes, turning, until cooked on all sides. Remove from heat; cool slightly. Cut each roll crosswise into 1/2-inch-thick slices. Insert a small wooden pick into each slice. Prepare Dipping Sauce and serve with chicken pinwheels.

MAKES ABOUT 36 PINWHEELS.

DIPPING SAUCE

In a 1-quart saucepan, combine chutney, peanut butter, broth, honey, red pepper flakes and garlic. Bring to a boil; simmer 5 minutes.

Munchy Sesame Wings

It takes twenty to twenty-two round sesame crackers to make enough crumbs to coat the chicken wings.

1 tablespoon soy sauce
1 clove garlic, crushed
1/3 cup Dijon mustard
2 tablespoons margarine or butter, melted
1/4 teaspoon salt
1/8 teaspoon pepper
1 cup sesame-cracker crumbs
1 teaspoon grated fresh gingerroot or 1/4 teaspoon ground ginger
20 chicken-wing drumettes or 10 chicken wings divided in half

Preheat oven to 350F (175C). Combine soy sauce, garlic, mustard, margarine or butter, salt and pepper in a small bowl. Combine cracker crumbs and ginger in a shallow bowl. Brush soy-sauce mixture on chicken wings. Roll sauce-coated wing pieces in crumbs to lightly coat.

Place crumb-coated wing pieces in a single layer on a 15 × 10-inch jelly-roll pan. Bake 45 to 50 minutes or until golden brown. Cool in pan 5 minutes. Serve warm.

MAKES 20 WING PIECES.

Chicken Dijon Tidbits

These skewered chicken tidbits have a superb flavor.

2 whole chicken breasts, skinned and boned
1/4 cup margarine or butter
2 teaspoons Dijon mustard
1 clove garlic, crushed
1 tablespoon minced fresh parsley
1 teaspoon fresh lemon juice
1/8 teaspoon salt
1/4 cup fine dry bread crumbs
1/4 cup (about 1 oz.) freshly grated Parmesan cheese

Cut chicken breasts into 3/4-inch cubes. Melt margarine or butter in a medium skillet over medium heat. Stir in mustard, garlic, parsley, lemon juice and salt. Add chicken; sauté over medium heat 5 to 10 minutes, turning chicken until lightly browned on all sides.

Sprinkle with bread crumbs and Parmesan cheese; toss until chicken is evenly coated. Spoon into a flat serving dish and serve warm with small wooden or plastic picks.

MAKES 70 TO 75 APPETIZERS.

Tahitian Sunset Roll-Ups

Crisp, emerald chicken-filled morsels are sure to please your guests.

2 whole chicken breasts, halved
2 cups chicken broth or bouillon
4 teaspoons curry powder
24 to 32 small lettuce leaves
1 cup shredded sweetened coconut, toasted (page 124)

TAHITIAN DIP

1 cup sour cream
2 tablespoons finely chopped peanuts
1/4 cup finely chopped chutney

Combine chicken breasts, broth or bouillon and curry powder in a medium saucepan over medium heat. Bring to a boil, reduce heat and simmer about 25 minutes or until chicken is tender. Refrigerate chicken in broth until cool.

Remove chicken breasts from broth. Remove and discard skin and bones. Cut each half breast lengthwise into 6 to 8 strips. Place each strip of chicken across one side of each lettuce leaf. Fold ends of lettuce over chicken; roll up. Secure with a wooden pick, if necessary. Refrigerate at least 1 hour.

Prepare Tahitian Dip. Spoon coconut into a small bowl. On a tray or large platter, arrange lettuce-wrapped chicken around dip and coconut. To serve, dip chicken rolls into Tahitian Dip, then into coconut.

MAKES 24 TO 32 APPETIZER SERVINGS.

TAHITIAN DIP

Combine sour cream, peanuts and chutney in a small bowl.

Chicken Saté

This spicy chicken appetizer is equally impressive when made with lean boneless pork cubes.

2 tablespoons vegetable oil
1 clove garlic, crushed
1 tomato, peeled, seeded and chopped
1/4 cup chunky peanut butter
1 cup chicken broth or bouillon
1/4 teaspoon salt
1/2 teaspoon crushed red pepper flakes
1 pound boneless, skinless chicken breasts

Heat oil and garlic in a small skillet over medium heat. Stir in tomato, peanut butter, broth or bouillon, salt and pepper flakes. Simmer about 10 minutes, stirring occasionally; set aside to cool.

Cut chicken into 3/4- to 1-inch pieces. Thread 3 pieces onto each of 10 or 11 (4-inch) bamboo skewers. Arrange in a 12 × 7-inch baking pan. Pour peanut butter mixture over skewered chicken; cover and refrigerate 5 to 6 hours.

Remove chicken from marinade, reserving marinade. Place rack 3 to 4 inches from heat source. Preheat broiler or grill. Broil chicken in oven or grill 4 to 5 minutes or until browned. Brush with reserved marinade; turn and broil other side about 2 minutes or until browned and tender. Serve hot.

Makes 10 to 11 appetizer servings.

All-American Turkey Meatballs

We like this updated version of ever-popular meatballs because it is lighter than the original dish. Cranberry sauce keeps it moist and flavorful.

1 pound ground turkey
1 egg, beaten slightly
1/2 cup soft bread crumbs
3/4 cup jellied cranberry sauce
1/4 cup milk
1 tablespoon finely chopped fresh parsley
1/2 teaspoon salt
1/4 cup steak sauce
1/8 teaspoon ground allspice
1 tablespoon minced chives
1 tablespoon white wine

Preheat oven to 375F (190C). Combine turkey, egg, bread crumbs, 1/4 cup of the cranberry sauce, milk, parsley and salt in a large bowl. Shape mixture into 1 1/4-inch meatballs.

Arrange meatballs in a single layer on a broiler pan. Bake 15 to 20 minutes or until cooked through. Arrange in a serving dish.

Heat remaining 1/2 cup cranberry sauce, steak sauce and allspice until melted in a small saucepan. Stir in chives and wine. Spoon sauce over meatballs. Serve with small picks.

MAKES ABOUT 50 MEATBALLS.

Easy Barbecued Turkey Cubes

Use spicy barbecue sauce or add a little hot pepper sauce if you enjoy spicy food.

1 (8-oz.) can jellied cranberry sauce
1/2 cup prepared barbecue sauce
1/8 teaspoon ground allspice
1/2 teaspoon grated orange peel
3 cups (1-inch) cubes cooked turkey

Heat cranberry sauce, barbecue sauce, allspice and orange peel in a chafing dish, stirring occasionally. Stir in cubed turkey; heat 10 minutes or until hot. Serve warm with small wooden or plastic picks.

MAKES ABOUT 45 APPETIZERS.

Turkey Brochettes

Cut turkey into larger pieces for a heartier snack.

2 cups (1/2- to 3/4-inch) cubes cooked turkey
1/4 cup vegetable oil
1/4 cup apricot jam
1/2 cup ketchup
1 teaspoon grated onion
1 teaspoon Worcestershire sauce
1/4 teaspoon salt
3 to 4 drops hot pepper sauce

Thread 3 or 4 turkey cubes on each of 12 to 15 (4-inch) bamboo skewers. Place in a 12 × 7-inch baking dish; set aside.

Combine oil, jam, ketchup, onion, Worcestershire sauce, salt and hot pepper sauce in a small bowl. Pour over skewered turkey pieces. Cover and refrigerate 6 hours or overnight to blend flavors. Drain, reserving sauce.

Place rack 3 to 4 inches from heat source. Preheat broiler or grill. Broil in oven or on grill until browned and crisp on edges, about 3 minutes. Brush with sauce; turn and brown other side.

MAKES 12 TO 15 APPETIZER SERVINGS.

Layered Polenta Fish

Be sure to reserve one-half the picante sauce to enhance the finished dish.

8 ounces fish fillets, about 1/2 inch thick
1 (8-oz.) jar picante sauce
1 1/2 cups chicken broth
1 tablespoon margarine or butter
3/4 cup yellow cornmeal
3 ounces (3/4 cup) Monterey Jack cheese, shredded

Preheat oven to 350F (175C). Place fish in a baking dish. Top with 1/2 cup picante sauce. Bake, uncovered, about 20 minutes or until fish flakes easily. Break fish into bite-size pieces while still in baking dish; drain, discarding liquid. Set aside.

Line an 8-inch round cake pan with foil; grease foil. Combine broth, margarine or butter and cornmeal in a 2- to 3-quart saucepan. Bring to a boil over medium-high heat. Reduce heat and simmer, stirring occasionally, 5 minutes or until thickened. Spread almost half of the cornmeal mixture in prepared pan. Top with reserved drained fish, pressing down lightly. Sprinkle with half of the cheese. Spread remaining cornmeal mixture over cheese. Top with remaining cheese.

Bake 10 minutes or until cheese melts. Let stand 5 minutes, then cut into wedges. Serve with remaining picante sauce.

MAKES ABOUT 6 TO 8 APPETIZERS.

Bouillabaisse-Style Seafood Bites

Traditional bouillabaisse ingredients flavor this dish.

2 tablespoons olive oil or vegetable oil
1 small onion, chopped
1 clove garlic, crushed
1/4 teaspoon dried basil leaves
1/4 teaspoon dried marjoram leaves
1/2 teaspoon salt
1/4 teaspoon pepper
1 teaspoon fresh lemon juice
Pinch of saffron
1 (8-oz.) can tomato sauce
1 cup chicken broth or bouillon
8 ounces scallops
8 ounces peeled medium shrimp, raw, or cubed raw lobster

Heat oil in a large skillet over medium heat. Add onion; sauté until softened. Add garlic, basil, marjoram, salt, pepper, lemon juice, saffron, tomato sauce and broth or bouillon. Simmer, uncovered, over medium-low heat 10 minutes.

If scallops are large, cut them into 1/2-inch cubes. Add scallops and shrimp or lobster to sauce. Cook, stirring occasionally, about 5 minutes until seafood is fork-tender. Turn into a chafing dish or a medium, heatproof bowl on a hot tray. Furnish wooden or plastic picks or small forks to pick up seafood.

MAKES ABOUT 3 CUPS.

Double-Salmon Pinwheels

The exact yield depends on the size and shape of each slice of smoked salmon. Our tests are based on slices that average about 6 × 2 inches.

6 ounces thinly sliced smoked salmon (lox)	1 teaspoon chopped fresh dill
1/4 cup sour cream	Dash hot pepper sauce
1 hard-cooked egg, coarsely chopped	2 tablespoons margarine or butter, melted
1 teaspoon chopped chives	Black caviar
1 teaspoon prepared horseradish	Sprigs of fresh dill
1 teaspoon fresh lemon juice	Lemon-peel curls

Set aside 4 slices of salmon. Coarsely chop remaining salmon. In a food processor, combine chopped salmon, sour cream, hard-cooked egg, chives, horseradish, lemon juice, chopped dill, hot pepper sauce and margarine or butter. Process until mixture is almost smooth.

Cut reserved salmon slices in half crosswise, forming 8 (3 × 2-inch) pieces. Spread each piece with salmon mixture. Roll up lengthwise. Refrigerate at least 1 hour.

Just before serving, cut each roll crosswise in halves or thirds. Set each piece on a cut end. Top with a dab of caviar, a fresh sprig of dill and a lemon-peel curl.

MAKES 16 TO 24 SERVINGS.

Sesame-Crab Dumplings

Pinch tiny pleats in top of filled wonton wrappers and you'll end up with little dumplings shaped like a vase.

7 ounces fresh, frozen or canned crabmeat
1/2 teaspoon grated gingerroot
1 egg, beaten slightly
2 tablespoons plum sauce
2 tablespoons chopped green onion
1/4 cup chopped canned water chestnuts
1/4 teaspoon salt
1/8 teaspoon pepper
20 to 25 (3-inch) round wonton wrappers
1 teaspoon white sesame seeds, toasted (see Note, page 109), or black sesame seeds

Flake crabmeat in a small bowl. Blend in ginger, egg, plum sauce, green onion, water chestnuts, salt and pepper. Spoon about 2 teaspoons crab mixture into center of each wonton wrapper. Bring edge up around filling on all sides, pinching pleats as you go. Leave top open. Sprinkle top with toasted sesame seeds or black sesame seeds.

Bring about 2 cups water to a boil in a wok or 12-inch skillet. Arrange dumplings, open side up, on a steamer rack in wok or skillet. Cover; steam over low heat 10 to 12 minutes or until wonton wrappers are translucent. Serve warm.

MAKES 20 TO 25 SERVINGS.

Crab-Stuffed Artichoke Bottoms

A sumptuous dish for special celebrations! Look for cans of water-packed artichoke bottoms.

1 1/2 tablespoons margarine or butter
1 tablespoon all-purpose flour
1/4 teaspoon dry mustard
1/4 teaspoon salt
1/8 teaspoon white pepper
Pinch ground red pepper
3 tablespoons chopped green onions
1/4 cup half and half
1/8 teaspoon Worcestershire sauce
1 tablespoon sherry
1 egg white, beaten until frothy
2 teaspoons finely chopped green bell pepper
6 ounces lump crabmeat, cut into small pieces
2 (14-oz.) cans artichoke bottoms, drained and rinsed
1 tablespoon margarine or butter, melted
Paprika

Preheat oven to 450F (230C). Melt 1 1/2 tablespoons margarine or butter in a medium saucepan; stir in flour, dry mustard, salt, white pepper and red pepper. Add green onions. Gradually stir in half and half; bring to a boil, stirring constantly. Remove from heat; stir in Worcestershire sauce, sherry and egg white. Fold in bell pepper and crabmeat.

Brush artichoke bottoms with melted margarine or butter. Spoon about 1 tablespoon crabmeat mixture into each artichoke bottom. Sprinkle lightly with paprika. Place on a baking sheet. Bake, uncovered, 10 minutes or until hot.

MAKES 12 TO 16 SERVINGS.

Butterflied Bayou Shrimp

Have lots of paper napkins ready for your guests to use as they shell their own shrimp.

1 pound medium raw shrimp in shells
1/4 cup margarine or butter
1/4 cup vegetable oil
2 tablespoons fresh lemon juice
1/4 teaspoon salt
1/4 teaspoon pepper
2 tablespoons prepared barbecue sauce
1 bay leaf, crumbled
1 clove garlic, crushed
1/2 teaspoon dried basil leaves
1/2 teaspoon dried rosemary leaves
1/2 teaspoon paprika
1/2 teaspoon crushed red pepper flakes

Butterfly shrimp by cutting lengthwise down back, without cutting all the way through. Do not remove shells. Melt margarine or butter in a large skillet over medium heat; add shrimp. Sauté 3 to 4 minutes, stirring occasionally, until shrimp begin to turn pink. Add remaining ingredients. Simmer over low heat 3 to 4 minutes, stirring occasionally. Remove from heat.

Cover and let stand about 5 minutes. Spoon shrimp and sauce into a large serving bowl.

MAKES 35 TO 40 APPETIZER SERVINGS.

Pickled Shrimp

Serve with wooden or plastic picks or small forks to pick up shrimp.

1 pound medium raw shrimp
1 tablespoon pickling spices
1 tablespoon Dijon mustard
1 teaspoon prepared horseradish
1/4 cup vegetable oil

1/2 teaspoon salt
1/4 teaspoon celery salt
1/2 cup white-wine vinegar
2 green onions, sliced

Peel and devein shrimp; discard shells. Add shrimp and pickling spices to a 2-quart saucepan. Add enough water to cover and bring to a boil over high heat. Reduce heat to medium and simmer about 2 minutes. Strain through a wire strainer. Add shrimp and spices to a medium bowl.

Combine mustard, horseradish, oil, salt, celery salt, vinegar and onions in a small bowl. Pour over shrimp. Cover and refrigerate 6 hours or overnight. Serve cold.

MAKES 35 TO 45 APPETIZERS.

Gingered Shrimp Balls

The mixture has a tendency to stick to your fingers when forming the shrimp balls. It's best to chill the mixture in the refrigerator for about an hour; then dip your hands in cold water before shaping it into balls.

1 pound medium raw shrimp, peeled and deveined
1 tablespoon grated gingerroot
1/2 cup canned sliced water chestnuts
2 tablespoons cornstarch
1 tablespoon soy sauce
1 teaspoon sesame oil
2 tablespoons chopped green onion
1/4 cup loosely packed fresh cilantro leaves
1 egg white
Hot mustard (optional)

Combine shrimp, ginger, water chestnuts, cornstarch, soy sauce, sesame oil, green onion, cilantro and egg white in a food processor. Process until finely chopped but not pureed. If time permits, cover and refrigerate 1 hour.

Lightly oil a heatproof plate. Shape shrimp mixture into 1 1/2-inch balls; place balls on prepared plate. Place in top of a steamer. Pour 2 cups boiling water in bottom of steamer. Cover; steam 12 minutes or until shrimp balls are firm. If steamer is not large enough to accommodate the entire recipe, steam 1/2 the recipe at a time. Serve with hot mustard, if desired.

MAKES 25 TO 30 SHRIMP BALLS.

Curried Scallops and Fruit Kabobs

Bay scallops are about 1/2 inch in diameter, but sea scallops are much larger—about 1 1/2 inches in diameter. If your scallops are large, cut them into 3/4-inch pieces for ease in cooking and eating.

1 pound scallops
1/4 fresh pineapple, peeled and cut into 1-inch cubes
2 firm, green-tipped bananas, peeled and cut crosswise into 1-inch slices

2 tablespoons pineapple or orange juice
1/4 cup margarine or butter, melted
2 tablespoons finely chopped chutney
1/2 teaspoon curry powder

Preheat broiler or grill. Place rack 5 to 8 inches from heat source. If broiling, place a rack in a large broiler pan; set aside.

Thread scallops, pineapple and banana pieces alternately onto 18 to 22 (4- to 6-inch) skewers.

Combine juice, margarine or butter, chutney and curry powder in a small bowl. Brush skewered fruit and scallops with sauce. Arrange skewered fruit and scallops on rack in broiler pan or on grill rack. Broil each side 2 to 3 minutes until scallops are firm; serve hot.

MAKES 18 TO 22 APPETIZERS.

Little Savory Bites

Skewered Szechuan-Style Barbecued Pork

If you use bamboo skewers, soak them in water several hours ahead of time to keep them from burning.

1 pound pork tenderloin
36 (2-inch) green onion pieces
1 (8-oz.) package (24 ears) frozen baby corn, thawed
1 cup hoisin sauce
1/2 cup plum sauce
1 teaspoon hot chili oil
1 teaspoon sesame oil
2 tablespoons soy sauce
2 tablespoons dry sherry wine
2 tablespoons honey
4 cloves garlic, finely chopped

Line a baking sheet with foil; set aside. Cut tenderloin in half crosswise, then lengthwise into 1/4-inch-thick slices. Pound slices gently between 2 pieces of waxed paper to 1/8-inch thickness. Cut each strip in half lengthwise again to approximately 5 × 1 1/2 inches.

Place a green onion piece at narrow end of a pork strip; roll up like a jelly roll. Alternately thread 3 pork rolls with 2 baby ears of corn onto a 6-inch skewer. Arrange on foil-lined baking sheet.

Combine hoisin sauce, plum sauce, chili oil, sesame oil, soy sauce, sherry wine, honey and garlic in a small bowl; blend well. Brush mixture over pork and corn; let stand 1 hour.

Preheat grill. Cook about 4 inches from heat source 5 to 7 minutes or until browned on both sides, brushing with sauce once or twice during cooking. Bring remaining sauce to a boil over medium heat. Serve pork and corn warm with remaining sauce for dipping.

MAKES 12 SERVINGS.

Mexican Pork Cubes

Pick up guacamole or salsa at the deli, or prepare your favorite recipe.

2 tablespoons vegetable oil
1 large clove garlic, pressed
1/4 teaspoon dried leaf oregano, crushed
1/2 teaspoon ground cumin
1/2 teaspoon salt
1/2 teaspoon pepper
1/2 teaspoon grated orange peel
1 tablespoon fresh orange juice
1 pound boneless pork, trimmed and cut into 1 1/2-inch cubes
Guacamole or salsa, for dipping

Combine vegetable oil, garlic, oregano, cumin, salt, pepper, orange peel and orange juice in a medium bowl; blend well. Add pork cubes, turning to coat evenly with mixture. Cover and refrigerate 3 to 4 hours to marinate.

Preheat broiler. Remove pork cubes from marinade; place on an ungreased baking pan. Discard marinade. Broil pork 4 to 5 inches from heat source 3 minutes; turn pork. Broil another 3 minutes or until lightly browned and pork is no longer pink when slashed. Transfer pork to a heated platter. Serve hot on small wooden picks with guacamole or salsa for dipping.

MAKES 18 TO 20 PIECES.

Indonesian Pork Saté

You'll need 6-inch bamboo skewers for these spicy mini-kabobs.

1 1/2 pounds lean boneless pork
1 cup roasted, salted peanuts
1/2 cup chopped green onions
2 tablespoons fresh lemon juice
2 tablespoons honey
1/4 cup soy sauce

1 clove garlic, chopped
1 teaspoon coriander seeds
1/2 teaspoon crushed dried red peppers
1/2 cup chicken broth or bouillon
1/4 cup butter, melted

Trim and discard fat from pork. Cut pork into 1-inch cubes. Thread 3 or 4 cubes onto each of 20 to 25 (6-inch) bamboo skewers. Layer skewered pork in an 8-inch-square baking dish; set aside.

Combine peanuts, onions, lemon juice, honey, soy sauce, garlic, coriander seeds and red peppers in a blender. Blend until almost smooth. Add broth or bouillon and butter. Blend 3 to 4 seconds to combine. Pour over skewered pork cubes. Marinate 6 hours or overnight in refrigerator.

Preheat broiler or grill. Drain pork; reserve marinade. Place rack 5 to 8 inches from heat source. Place a wire rack in a broiler pan or on grill. Arrange marinated pork on rack. Broil until browned and crisp, about 5 minutes. Turn and brush with marinade; broil until browned on all sides, 4 to 5 minutes. Arrange on a large platter; serve hot.

MAKES 20 TO 25 APPETIZERS.

Meatballs with Luau Sauce

The perfect dish for a Hawaiian party around the pool, these meatballs can be made in advance and reheated in the sauce just before serving.

1 pound lean ground pork
1 (8-oz.) can water chestnuts, drained and finely chopped
1/4 cup finely chopped green onions
1/2 teaspoon salt
1/2 teaspoon Worcestershire sauce
1/3 cup fine dry bread crumbs
1 egg, beaten

LUAU SAUCE

1 cup unsweetened pineapple juice
1/4 cup dry white wine
1/2 cup chicken broth or bouillon
2 tablespoons light brown sugar
2 teaspoons finely chopped crystallized ginger
1 tablespoon cornstarch
1 tablespoon soy sauce

Preheat oven to 375F (190C). Combine pork, water chestnuts, onions, salt, Worcestershire sauce and bread crumbs in a medium bowl. Use a fork to stir in egg until thoroughly combined. Shape mixture into 1-inch balls. Arrange on a rack in broiler pan. Bake 30 to 35 minutes or until lightly browned throughout. Drain and discard drippings. Prepare Luau Sauce.

Arrange cooked meatballs in a chafing dish or heatproof dish on a hot tray. Pour sauce over meatballs; serve hot.

MAKES 60 TO 65 MEATBALLS.

LUAU SAUCE

Combine pineapple juice, wine, chicken broth or bouillon, brown sugar and ginger in a small saucepan. Bring to a boil over medium heat. Dissolve cornstarch in soy sauce; stir into hot pineapple mixture. Cook, stirring, over medium heat until slightly thickened.

Little Savory Bites

Oriental-Style Baby-Back Ribs

Baby-back ribs are smaller and more tender than regular ribs.

2 1/4 pounds baby-back pork ribs
Salt
Pepper
2 tablespoons honey
2 tablespoons soy sauce
1 tablespoon grated gingerroot

1 clove garlic, crushed
2 tablespoons hoisin sauce
1 tablespoon fresh lemon juice
2 tablespoons finely chopped green onion

Preheat oven to 350F (175C). Cut meat into individual ribs; place in a shallow baking pan. Season with salt and pepper. Cover with foil. Bake 35 to 40 minutes or until almost done.

Uncover ribs; increase oven temperature to 425F (220C). Meanwhile, in a medium saucepan, combine honey, soy sauce, ginger, garlic, hoisin sauce, lemon juice and green onion; simmer 5 minutes over low heat. Brush tops of cooked ribs with sauce; bake 10 minutes. Turn, brush other side with sauce; bake ribs another 5 minutes or until glazed.

MAKES 20 TO 25 RIB PIECES.

Plum-Glazed Spareribs

To achieve the delicious plum flavor without a lot of fuss, plum jelly is used as the base for the glaze.

3 to 3 1/2 pounds pork spareribs
1/4 cup soy sauce
2 tablespoons honey
2 tablespoons fresh lemon juice
1 clove garlic, crushed
1/4 cup dry white wine

1 cup plum jelly
2 tablespoons vinegar
2 tablespoons ketchup
1/4 cup sesame seeds, toasted
   (see Note, page 109)

Have your butcher cut ribs crosswise. Cut between bones to separate ribs. Place separated ribs in a large glass baking dish; set aside.

Combine soy sauce, honey, lemon juice, garlic and wine in a small bowl. Pour over ribs. Cover and marinate 6 hours or overnight in the refrigerator.

Preheat oven to 375F (190C). Drain ribs; discard marinade. Arrange marinated ribs in a 15 × 10-inch baking pan with sides. Cover and bake 45 minutes.

Meanwhile, combine jelly, vinegar and ketchup in a small saucepan. Stir over low heat until jelly melts. Brush sauce over baked ribs. Bake 10 minutes, uncovered. Turn ribs; brush with sauce. Sprinkle with sesame seeds. Bake, uncovered, 10 minutes or until glazed. Arrange baked ribs on a large plate; serve hot.

MAKES 30 TO 35 APPETIZERS.

Chinese Barbecued Riblets

Chinese five-spice powder and hoisin sauce are available in Asian food markets.

3 pounds pork spareribs
1/2 cup soy sauce
1 clove garlic, crushed
1/2 cup hoisin sauce
1/2 cup dry white wine
1/2 teaspoon ground ginger
1/2 teaspoon Chinese five-spice powder
3 or 4 drops red food coloring (optional)

Have your butcher cut ribs crosswise. Cut between bones to separate ribs. Add ribs to a large saucepan and cover with lightly salted water. Cover and simmer 30 minutes over medium-low heat. Drain; place cooked ribs in a large glass bowl. Set aside.

Combine soy sauce, garlic, hoisin sauce, wine, ginger, five-spice powder and red food coloring, if using. Pour over drained ribs. Cover and marinate 3 to 4 hours in the refrigerator, turning occasionally.

Drain ribs; reserve marinade. Preheat broiler or grill. Place rack in broiler pan or on grill. Arrange drained meat on rack. Broil until browned and crisp about 10 minutes, turning once and brushing with marinade. Arrange on a platter; serve hot.

MAKES 30 TO 35 APPETIZERS.

Sunset Ham Balls

Make up ham balls ahead of time and add them to the sauce just before serving.

1 pound lean cooked ham
1 egg
1 cup soft bread crumbs
2 tablespoons chopped green onions
1 teaspoon minced parsley
1/8 teaspoon seasoned salt
1/2 teaspoon prepared mustard
1/2 cup barbecue sauce
1 (10-oz.) jar apricot-pineapple jam

Preheat oven to 350F (175C). Grind ham in a food grinder or food processor; set aside. Beat egg slightly in a medium bowl. Stir in bread crumbs, green onions, parsley, seasoned salt and mustard. Stir in ground ham. Shape into 1-inch balls.

Arrange ham balls on a rack in a broiler pan. Bake about 15 minutes or until lightly browned.

Combine barbecue sauce and jam in a large skillet or stovetop-to-table casserole dish; stir over medium heat until blended. Add cooked ham balls; heat until bubbly. Serve hot in casserole dish or spoon into a chafing dish.

MAKES 35 TO 40 HAM BALLS.

No-Liver Chutney Rumaki

There is no liver in this spicy fruit version of traditional rumaki.

1 pound sliced bacon
1 tablespoon prepared mustard
2 tablespoons light brown sugar

1/4 cup fruit chutney
1 (8-oz.) can water chestnuts, drained

Preheat oven to 400F (205C). Cook bacon over medium heat until most of the fat is removed but bacon is still soft. Drain on paper towels. Lightly spread one side of each bacon slice with mustard. Sprinkle evenly with brown sugar; set aside.

Remove fruit from chutney and very finely chop. Return chopped fruit to chutney syrup. Dip each water chestnut into chutney. With coated side up, wrap a bacon slice around each water chestnut; secure ends of bacon with small wooden picks. Arrange bacon-wrapped water chestnuts in a 13 × 9-inch baking pan. Bake 5 to 10 minutes or until bacon is crisp. Serve warm.

MAKES 14 TO 16 APPETIZERS.

Korean-Style Beef and Mushrooms

For economy, use smaller pieces of meat and several fresh pineapple chunks on each skewer.

1 pound boneless beef top sirloin steak
15 to 20 small mushrooms
2 tablespoons vegetable oil
1/4 cup soy sauce
1 clove garlic, crushed
1/4 cup minced onion
1/8 teaspoon pepper
1 (1/4-inch) slice gingerroot, finely chopped, or 1/4 teaspoon ground ginger
1 teaspoon honey

Have your butcher cut steak into 15 to 20 very thin slices or partially freeze steak and cut into very thin slices. Thread meat onto 15 to 20 (6-inch) bamboo skewers by pushing skewers in and out of each meat slice. Top each skewer with a mushroom; set aside.

Combine oil, soy sauce, garlic, onion, pepper, ginger and honey in a 9 × 5-inch loaf pan. Place skewered meat in marinade, turning to coat all sides. Cover and refrigerate 6 hours or overnight, turning occasionally.

Preheat broiler or grill. Drain meat, reserving marinade. Place rack 5 to 8 inches from heat source. Broil skewered meat about 2 minutes, basting several times with reserved marinade. Turn and baste with marinade; broil about 2 minutes or until evenly browned. Serve hot.

MAKES 15 TO 20 APPETIZERS.

Teriyaki Roll-Ups

Partially frozen beef holds its shape and is easier to cut into thin slices.

1/3 cup soy sauce
2 tablespoons honey
1/4 teaspoon ground ginger
1 clove garlic, crushed
1 teaspoon grated onion

1/4 cup dry white wine
12 ounces boneless beef top sirloin
  or fillet
1 (8-oz.) can water chestnuts, drained

Combine soy sauce, honey, ginger, garlic, onion and wine in a medium shallow bowl; set aside. Cut beef on diagonal into very thin slices. Cut water chestnuts in half. Wrap 1 slice meat around each water chestnut half. Secure with a wooden pick. Marinate in soy sauce mixture in the refrigerator 1 hour.

Preheat broiler. Place oven rack 5 to 8 inches from heat source. Remove marinated roll-ups from marinade, discarding marinade; arrange on broiler pan. Broil beef 3 to 4 minutes or until evenly browned, turning once or twice. Serve hot.

MAKES 40 TO 45 APPETIZERS.

Beef Yakitori

These tasty morsels are similar to one of Japan's favorite beef dishes.

1/2 cup soy sauce
2 tablespoons fresh lemon juice
2 tablespoons sugar
1 clove garlic, crushed
1/2 teaspoon ground ginger

2 tablespoons vegetable oil
1 teaspoon sesame seeds
2 green onions, finely chopped
1 pound beef sirloin, thinly sliced

Combine soy sauce, lemon juice, sugar, garlic, ginger, oil, sesame seeds and onions in a 9 × 5-inch loaf pan. Thread beef onto 18 to 20 (6-inch) bamboo skewers by pushing a skewer in and out of each beef slice. Place skewered meat in marinade, turning to coat all sides. Cover and refrigerate 3 to 4 hours.

Preheat broiler. Drain beef, discarding marinade, and arrange skewered beef on a broiler pan or ungreased baking sheet with sides. Place oven rack 5 to 8 inches from heat source. Broil meat 1 1/2 to 2 minutes; turn and broil about 1 minute. Serve hot.

MAKES 18 TO 20 APPETIZERS.

Classic Sweet and Sour Meatballs

Serve these savory meatballs in a piquant sauce for your cocktail buffet main dish.

1 egg, slightly beaten
1/3 cup milk
1/2 cup soft bread crumbs
1/2 teaspoon salt
1/8 teaspoon pepper
1/4 teaspoon ground sage
1/4 cup minced onion
1 pound lean ground beef

Sweet and Sour Sauce

1 (8-oz.) can sliced pineapple
2 tablespoons cornstarch
2 tablespoons soy sauce
1 cup chicken broth or bouillon
1/4 cup vinegar
1/4 cup honey
1 green bell pepper, cut into 1-inch squares

Preheat oven to 350F (175C). Combine egg, milk, bread crumbs, salt, pepper, sage and onion in a medium bowl. Stir in ground beef. Shape into 1-inch balls. Arrange on a rack in a broiler pan. Bake 15 to 20 minutes or until lightly browned. Drain and discard drippings. Prepare Sweet and Sour Sauce.

To serve, arrange meatballs in a chafing dish or heatproof bowl on a hot tray. Pour sauce evenly over meatballs. Serve warm.

MAKES ABOUT 55 MEATBALLS.

Sweet and Sour Sauce

Drain pineapple juice into a small saucepan; set aside. Cut pineapple into 3/4-inch pieces; set aside. Stir cornstarch into reserved pineapple juice until dissolved. Stir in soy sauce, broth or bouillon, vinegar and honey. Cook, stirring, over medium-low heat until thickened and translucent. Stir in pineapple chunks and bell pepper squares. Cook 1 minute.

Crunchy Meatballs

You'll enjoy these plain, but they are even better served with teriyaki sauce.

1 pound lean ground beef	1 tablespoon soy sauce
8 ounces lean ground pork	1/4 teaspoon garlic salt
2 eggs, slightly beaten	1 (8-oz.) can water chestnuts, drained
1/2 teaspoon salt	and finely chopped
1/4 cup fine dry bread crumbs	1 cup teriyaki sauce (optional)

Preheat oven to 375F (190C). Combine beef, pork, eggs, salt, bread crumbs, soy sauce, garlic salt and water chestnuts in a medium bowl. Shape into 1-inch balls. Arrange on a rack in a broiler pan. Bake 15 to 18 minutes or until meatballs are browned. Drain and discard drippings.

Pour teriyaki sauce into a small bowl, if using. To serve, spear warm baked meatballs with small wooden picks; dip into teriyaki sauce, if desired.

MAKES ABOUT 75 MEATBALLS.

Beefy Mushroom Pinwheels

These are best when eaten within an hour or two after they're made. Sliced chipped beef from the deli or in jars may be substituted for the spiced beef.

1 tablespoon vegetable oil
3 ounces (1 cup) mushrooms, finely chopped
2 tablespoons chopped watercress
1/2 of a (1 1/4-oz.) envelope dry onion-soup mix (about 3 tablespoons)
3/4 cup sour cream
1 teaspoon prepared horseradish
2 ounces (about 10 thin slices) cooked spiced beef
Watercress sprigs, for garnish

Heat oil in a small skillet. Add mushrooms; sauté over medium heat until liquid evaporates, about 10 minutes. Remove from heat.

Stir in chopped watercress, dry onion-soup mix, sour cream and horseradish. Spread about 2 tablespoons mixture over each beef slice to within 1/4 inch of edges; gently roll up. Cover and refrigerate 1 hour. Cut each roll into 4 pieces. Garnish with watercress sprigs.

MAKES 40 PIECES.

Deli Party Carousel

Get out your prettiest tray for this party platter. It's an impressive idea for holiday parties or family reunions. Long, thin, Italian-style bread sticks are especially appealing; thin slices of roast beef make an interesting change.

2 tablespoons Dijon mustard
1/3 cup sour cream
1/3 cup mayonnaise
1 clove garlic, minced
1/4 teaspoon salt
1 teaspoon green peppercorns,
    drained and slightly crushed

8 to 10 slices salami
8 to 10 slices mortadella
8 to 10 slices cooked pastrami
24 to 30 bread sticks
Tomato rose, for garnish (optional)

Combine mustard, sour cream, mayonnaise, garlic and salt in a small bowl. Stir in peppercorns. Cover and refrigerate at least 1 hour.

Spread about 1 to 1 1/2 teaspoons mustard mixture on each slice of salami, mortadella and pastrami. Roll each around a bread stick. Arrange, seam side down, in a spoke design on a round tray. Place a tomato rose in center, if using.

MAKES 24 TO 30 SERVINGS.

Little Savory Bites

Toasted Almond and Brie Slices

Create this appetizer or snack tray and let your guests make their own favorite combination.

2 (4 1/2-oz.) packages Brie cheese
1 tablespoon all-purpose flour
1 egg, beaten slightly
1/4 cup fine dry bread crumbs
1/3 cup finely chopped almonds, toasted (see Note, page 205)

1 pear, thinly sliced and dipped in lemon juice, to serve
1 medium bunch of seedless grapes, to serve
Sesame crackers, to serve

Preheat oven to 400F (205C). Grease a baking sheet. Dip Brie cheese into flour, then into beaten egg, turning until all sides are evenly coated. Combine bread crumbs and almonds in a shallow bowl. Dip all sides of cheese into crumb mixture. Place on greased baking sheet. Bake 10 minutes or until browned. Cut cheese into thin slices. Serve with thin slices of pear, seedless grapes and sesame crackers.

MAKES 2 CHEESE ROUNDS.

Brie en Croûte

Pastry dough is easier to roll when it has been chilled at least one hour.

3/4 cup all-purpose flour
1 (3-oz.) package cream cheese, at room temperature
1/4 cup butter, at room temperature
1 (4 1/2-oz.) package Brie cheese
1/2 teaspoon sesame seeds

Sift flour into a medium bowl. Add cream cheese and butter and cut into flour with a pastry blender until particles resemble small peas. Shape into a ball. Wrap in foil or plastic wrap; refrigerate at least 1 hour.

Preheat oven to 400F (205C). Divide dough into 2 pieces. On a lightly floured surface, roll out each piece to about 1/8-inch thickness. Cut each piece into a 6-inch circle, reserving excess dough for trim. Place 1 circle of dough on an ungreased baking sheet. Place whole Brie cheese in center of dough; top with other pastry circle. Pinch pastry edges together to seal. Roll out excess dough. Cut 1 decorative design with a cookie cutter and about 10 small designs with hors d'oeuvre cutters. Place large cut-out on top of pastry and small cut-outs around side. Sprinkle with sesame seeds.

Bake 15 to 17 minutes or until golden brown. Let stand several minutes before cutting into small wedges. Serve warm.

MAKES 16 TO 18 APPETIZER SERVINGS.

Little Savory Bites

Dilly Cheese Cubes

Make these ahead, then refrigerate or freeze the soft-centered cubes and bake them later.

1 (8-oz.) loaf French bread, unsliced
1/2 cup butter
1 pound (4 cups) sharp Cheddar cheese, shredded
2 teaspoons dried dill weed
1 teaspoon Worcestershire sauce
1 tablespoon grated onion
2 eggs, slightly beaten

Remove crust from bread; reserve crusts for another purpose. Cut bread into 40 to 45 (1-inch) cubes; set aside. Add butter and cheese to a medium saucepan over low heat. Cook, stirring, until melted. Stir in dill weed, Worcestershire sauce and onion. Remove from heat and cool slightly. Use a whisk or electric mixer to beat in eggs.

Using a fork, dip each bread cube into hot cheese mixture, turning to coat all sides. Shake off excess sauce. Arrange coated cubes on an ungreased baking sheet. Refrigerate 1 to 2 days or freeze immediately. Store frozen cubes in airtight containers up to 6 months.

To serve, preheat oven to 350F (175C). Bake refrigerated cheese cubes 8 to 10 minutes; bake frozen cheese cubes 15 minutes. Serve hot.

MAKES 40 TO 45 APPETIZERS.

Bacon and Cheese Polenta Squares

This updated version of traditional Italian polenta is cut into small squares for easy handling.

1 tablespoon margarine or butter
1 cup chicken stock or bouillon
1/2 cup yellow cornmeal
1 to 2 jalapeño chiles, seeded and minced
1 small onion, chopped
1/4 teaspoon salt
1/8 teaspoon pepper
2 slices bacon, cooked and crumbled
2 tablespoons chopped fresh cilantro
2 eggs, beaten slightly
1/2 cup cooked whole-kernel corn
1 ounce (1/4 cup) Cheddar cheese, shredded

Preheat oven to 400F (205C). Line an 8-inch-square baking pan with foil; grease foil. Bring margarine or butter and stock to a boil in a medium saucepan over medium heat. Gradually pour in cornmeal, stirring constantly. Add jalapeño chile, onion, salt and pepper. Cook, stirring, over medium heat 5 minutes or until thick.

Remove from heat; stir in bacon, cilantro, eggs and corn. Spoon into prepared pan. Sprinkle with cheese. Bake 12 minutes or until cheese is bubbly. Remove from oven; let stand 5 to 10 minutes before cutting. Cut into 1-inch squares.

MAKES ABOUT 50 SQUARES.

Confetti Polenta Cups

They aren't difficult to make, but be sure to pour the cornmeal in very slowly to ensure a smooth mixture.

1 1/4 cups chicken stock or bouillon
1/2 cup yellow cornmeal
1/4 cup chopped red bell pepper, plus additional for garnish
2 tablespoons chopped green onion, plus additional for garnish
1 teaspoon Dijon mustard
1/4 teaspoon salt
1/8 teaspoon pepper
3 ounces (3/4 cup) Cheddar cheese, shredded
2 eggs, beaten slightly
1/2 cup sour cream

Preheat oven to 350F (175C). Grease 24 miniature muffin cups. Bring stock to a boil in a medium saucepan. Gradually stir in cornmeal, stirring constantly. Cook, stirring constantly, over medium heat 4 minutes or until very thick. Remove from heat. Stir in 1/4 cup bell pepper, 2 tablespoons green onion, mustard, salt, pepper and 1/2 cup cheese.

Combine eggs and sour cream; stir into cooked cornmeal mixture. Spoon mixture into prepared muffin cups. Sprinkle with remaining 1/4 cup Cheddar cheese.

Bake 20 minutes or until firm. Let stand in pan about 5 minutes. Loosen from sides; remove from pans. Garnish with additional chopped red bell pepper and green onion. Serve warm.

MAKES 24 POLENTA CUPS.

Mediterranean Sampler

Feta is a white, salty cheese originally from Greece but now available in many countries.

4 eggs
1/2 cup plain yogurt
1/4 teaspoon salt
2 green onions, finely chopped
1 tablespoon minced fresh parsley
1/4 cup crumbled feta cheese
1/4 cup (about 1 oz.) finely chopped pepperoni
1 tablespoon sesame seeds

Preheat oven to 350F (175C). Grease an 8-inch-square baking pan; set aside. Beat eggs in a medium bowl until pale and thickened. Stir in yogurt, salt, onions, parsley, cheese and pepperoni. Pour evenly into prepared pan. Sprinkle with sesame seeds. Bake 15 to 20 minutes or until just set. Cut into 8 horizontal rows and 7 or 8 vertical rows.

MAKES 56 TO 64 APPETIZERS.

Bacon Cheesecake

It has the shape of a pie but a texture that's more similar to a cheesecake.

2 tablespoons margarine or butter, at room temperature
3/4 cup fine dry bread crumbs
2 tablespoons freshly grated Parmesan cheese
4 slices bacon, chopped
2 green onions, chopped
8 ounces (1 cup) ricotta cheese, drained
3 to 4 ounces blue cheese
2 eggs
1 cup plain yogurt
1 clove garlic, crushed
1/8 teaspoon pepper
2 tablespoons pine nuts

Preheat oven to 350F (175C). Combine margarine or butter, bread crumbs and Parmesan cheese in a small bowl. Press on side and bottom of a 9-inch pie pan.

Cook bacon until almost done in a small skillet. Drain off and discard fat. Stir in green onions.

Beat ricotta cheese and blue cheese until well mixed; beat in eggs. Stir in yogurt, garlic, pepper and bacon and onions. Pour into crumb-lined pie pan. Sprinkle with pine nuts.

Bake about 35 to 45 minutes or until firm in center. Cool; cut into small wedges.

Makes 6 to 8 servings.

Mexican Pizza

This chile relleno–flavored pizza bakes firm without a separate crust if allowed to stand at least five minutes after baking.

1/4 cup all-purpose flour
1/4 teaspoon salt
1/4 cup margarine or butter, melted
4 eggs, slightly beaten
1 (4-oz.) can chopped green chiles, drained
8 ounces (1 cup) cottage cheese, drained
8 ounces (2 cups) Monterey Jack cheese, shredded

Preheat oven to 375F (190C). Grease a 12-inch pizza pan; set aside. Combine flour, salt and melted margarine or butter in a medium bowl. Stir in eggs, chiles, cottage cheese and Monterey Jack cheese. Pour evenly into greased pan.

Bake 15 to 20 minutes or until firm. Remove from oven; cool in pan 5 minutes. Cut into thin wedges.

MAKES 16 TO 18 WEDGES.

Beachcomber Quiche

This quiche contains the usual ingredients, but there's no crust to make!

3 eggs
1 (3-oz.) package cream cheese, at room temperature
8 ounces (1 cup) cottage cheese, drained
1/4 cup butter, softened
1/4 cup all-purpose flour
1/2 teaspoon baking powder
1/2 cup milk
4 ounces (1 cup) Cheddar cheese, grated
5 slices bacon, cooked, drained and crumbled

Preheat oven to 350F (175C). Grease a 9-inch pie pan; set aside. Beat eggs in a large bowl. Beat in cream cheese, cottage cheese and butter until almost smooth.

Combine flour and baking powder in a small bowl. Stir into egg mixture until blended. Beat in milk until thoroughly blended. Pour evenly into prepared pie pan. Sprinkle with Cheddar cheese and bacon.

Bake 30 to 40 minutes or until mixture is firm in center. Let stand 5 minutes. Cut into 12 to 15 small wedges; serve warm.

MAKES 12 TO 15 WEDGES.

Jalapeño Pickled Eggs

Red-wine vinegar gives eggs a pinkish-brown color. Substitute white-wine vinegar for off-white eggs. Add more jalapeño chiles if you enjoy very hot foods.

1 cup red-wine vinegar
1 cup water
1 teaspoon pickling spices
1 clove garlic, peeled
1 small onion, sliced
1/2 teaspoon salt
2 jalapeño chiles, quartered
6 hard-cooked eggs, peeled

Combine vinegar, water, pickling spices, garlic, onion, salt and jalapeño chiles in a nonaluminum saucepan. Bring to a boil; simmer 2 minutes. Place hard-cooked eggs in a heatproof glass dish; pour hot mixture over eggs. Cover and refrigerate at least 24 hours before serving. Drain and discard marinade. Cut eggs in halves or quarters, if desired.

MAKES 6 EGGS.

Basic Deviled Eggs

Select your favorite flavor combination from the variations listed below.

6 hard-cooked eggs, peeled
3 tablespoons mayonnaise
1/2 teaspoon prepared mustard
2 teaspoons white-wine vinegar

1/4 teaspoon salt
1/8 teaspoon pepper
1/8 teaspoon celery seeds (optional)
Chopped fresh parsley, for garnish

Cut hard-cooked eggs in half lengthwise. Remove egg yolks; set egg whites aside. Use a fork to mash egg yolks in a small bowl. Stir in mayonnaise, mustard, vinegar, salt, pepper and celery seeds, if using. Spoon yolk mixture evenly into egg white halves. Arrange on a small platter. Garnish with parsley.

MAKES 12 APPETIZERS.

VARIATIONS

CURRIED CHUTNEY EGGS

Cut 6 hard-cooked eggs in half lengthwise. Mash egg yolks; stir in 3 tablespoons mayonnaise, 1 tablespoon finely chopped chutney, 1/2 teaspoon curry powder and 1/4 teaspoon salt. Spoon evenly into egg white halves.

CAVIAR EGGS

Cut 6 hard-cooked eggs in half lengthwise. Mash egg yolks; stir in 2 tablespoons melted margarine or butter, 2 tablespoons sour cream, 2 teaspoons fresh lemon juice and 1/4 teaspoon grated onion. Spoon evenly into egg white halves. Sprinkle 1/4 teaspoon caviar on each egg half.

ANCHOVY EGGS

Cut 6 hard-cooked eggs in half lengthwise. Mash egg yolks; stir in 3 tablespoons melted unsalted butter, 1 1/2 teaspoons anchovy paste, 2 teaspoons fresh lemon juice and 1/8 teaspoon pepper. Spoon evenly into egg white halves.

Fresh Herbed Eggs

Cut 6 hard-cooked eggs in half lengthwise. Mash egg yolks; stir in 3 tablespoons mayonnaise, 2 teaspoons white-wine vinegar, 1/2 teaspoon minced fresh tarragon, 2 teaspoons minced watercress, 1 teaspoon minced fresh chives and 1/4 teaspoon salt. Spoon evenly into egg white halves. Garnish each with a watercress sprig.

Rosy Eggs

Cut 6 hard-cooked eggs in half lengthwise. Mash egg yolks; stir in 2 tablespoons sour cream, 4 teaspoons juice from pickled beets, 1/2 teaspoon prepared mustard, 1/4 teaspoon salt and 1/8 teaspoon celery seeds. Spoon evenly into egg white halves.

Bacon and Cheese Eggs

Cut 6 hard-cooked eggs in half lengthwise. Mash egg yolks; stir in 2 slices cooked and finely crumbled bacon, 1/4 cup grated Cheddar cheese, 3 tablespoons mayonnaise, 2 teaspoons white-wine vinegar and 1/8 teaspoon salt. Spoon evenly into egg white halves. Garnish with extra bits of crumbled bacon, if desired.

Smoky Deviled Eggs

Cut 6 hard-cooked eggs in half lengthwise. Mash egg yolks; stir in 1 teaspoon prepared mustard, 1/4 cup softened smoky cheese spread, 1 teaspoon minced parsley, 2 tablespoons milk and 1/8 teaspoon seasoned salt. Spoon evenly into egg white halves. Garnish with parsley sprigs.

Parma Eggs

Cut 6 hard-cooked eggs in half lengthwise. Mash egg yolks; stir in 1 tablespoon finely chopped sun-dried tomatoes in oil, 1 1/2 teaspoons sweet-hot mustard, 1/3 cup finely chopped prosciutto and 1/4 cup mayonnaise. Spoon evenly into egg white halves. Garnish with Italian parsley sprigs.

Pickled Eggs and Beets

These marinated eggs take on a beautiful beet-red color and spicy pickled flavor.

1 (16-oz.) can sliced beets
6 hard-cooked eggs, peeled
1 cup white-wine vinegar
2 tablespoons sugar

1 tablespoon pickling spices
1/2 teaspoon salt
1/8 teaspoon pepper
1 onion, thinly sliced

Drain beets, reserving liquid. Place beets and peeled eggs in a large heatproof bowl; set aside. Combine beet liquid, vinegar, sugar, pickling spices, salt, pepper and onion in a nonaluminum saucepan. Bring to a boil over medium heat; simmer about 2 minutes. Pour over beets and eggs; cover and refrigerate 24 hours.

Drain and discard marinade. Cut eggs in half lengthwise. Arrange egg halves, beets and onion on a platter or tray.

MAKES 12 ANTIPASTO SERVINGS.

Monterey Artichoke Bake

The tangy marinade from the artichokes is what gives this dish its zing.

2 (6-oz.) jars marinated artichoke hearts
1 small onion, finely chopped
1 clove garlic, crushed
4 eggs
1/4 cup fine dry bread crumbs
8 ounces (2 cups) Monterey Jack cheese, shredded
1/4 teaspoon dried basil leaves, crushed
1/4 teaspoon dried oregano leaves, crushed
1/8 teaspoon pepper
2 tablespoons finely chopped canned green chiles
Pimiento strips (optional)

Drain artichoke hearts, reserving 1 tablespoon marinade in a small saucepan. Finely chop artichoke hearts; set aside. Add onion and garlic to reserved marinade. Sauté, stirring occasionally, over medium heat until onion is soft, about 5 minutes.

Preheat oven to 325F (165C). Grease an 8-inch-square baking pan; set aside. Beat eggs in a medium bowl until foamy. Stir in chopped artichoke hearts, bread crumbs, cheese, basil, oregano, pepper, green chiles and sautéed onion mixture. Spoon into prepared baking pan.

Bake 25 to 30 minutes or until mixture is firm. Let stand 5 minutes. Cut into 25 to 30 small bars or squares. Garnish each piece with a strip of pimiento, if desired. Serve warm or cold.

MAKES 25 TO 30 APPETIZERS.

Venetian Crowns

The exact number of appetizers depends on the number of artichoke bottoms in each can, because the number varies slightly. Sliced stuffed olives provide an interesting garnish.

2 (13 3/4-oz.) cans artichoke bottoms, drained and rinsed
1 egg
1/4 cup (about 1 ounce) freshly grated Parmesan cheese
1/2 cup ricotta cheese, drained
2 tablespoons chopped fresh basil
2 tablespoons sun-dried tomatoes (oil packed), drained and chopped
16 slices (about 1 ounce) pepperoni sausage, finely chopped
2 tablespoons fine dry bread crumbs
10 pimiento-stuffed olives, sliced, for garnish

Preheat oven to 325F (165C). Grease a 12 × 8-inch baking dish. Arrange artichokes over bottom of dish. Beat egg in a medium bowl. Stir in Parmesan cheese, ricotta cheese, basil, tomatoes and pepperoni. Spoon into centers of artichoke bottoms. Sprinkle with bread crumbs.

Bake 20 to 25 minutes until cheeses melt. Garnish with olive slices. Serve hot.

MAKES ABOUT 12.

Dilled Beans and Carrots

These are an easy way to add color to your cocktail buffet table or antipasto tray.

4 medium carrots (about 3/4 lb.)
10 to 16 ounces fresh or
 frozen green beans
2 cups white-wine vinegar
1/4 cup honey

1 teaspoon dried dill weed
1 teaspoon pickling spices
1 clove garlic, crushed
1/2 cup water
1 tablespoon salt

Peel carrots; cut into sticks. If using fresh beans, remove ends; break in half. Thaw frozen beans.

Combine vinegar, honey, dill weed, pickling spices, garlic, water and salt in a nonaluminum saucepan. Bring to a boil over high heat. Carefully lower carrot sticks and broken beans into boiling mixture. Cover and simmer 10 minutes over low heat. Set aside to cool 10 minutes. Refrigerate 3 to 4 hours in marinade. Spoon into large serving dish, discarding marinade.

MAKES ABOUT 10 BUFFET SERVINGS.

Marinated Garbanzo Beans

For a special treat, serve this dish with sliced salami or pepperoni.

1/2 cup vegetable oil
1/2 cup red-wine vinegar
1/4 teaspoon garlic salt
1/2 teaspoon fines herbes
2 tablespoons minced fresh parsley

2 tablespoons minced fresh chives
1/4 teaspoon salt
1/8 teaspoon pepper
2 (15-oz.) cans garbanzo beans, drained and rinsed

Combine oil, vinegar, garlic salt, fines herbes, parsley, chives, salt and pepper in a medium bowl. Stir to blend. Add drained beans; cover and refrigerate 6 hours or overnight. Drain, discarding marinade; arrange on an antipasto tray.

MAKES 4 CUPS.

French-Style Bean Rounds

This is an Americanized version of a popular French "street food" that probably originated in North Africa.

1 (15-oz.) can kidney beans, drained
4 tablespoons all-purpose flour
1 tablespoon vegetable oil
1/3 cup water
1 clove garlic, crushed
1/4 teaspoon chili powder
1/4 teaspoon salt
1/8 teaspoon pepper
Vegetable oil, for frying
Grated cheese (optional)

Combine well-drained beans, flour, 1 tablespoon oil, water, garlic, chili powder, salt and pepper in a blender or food processor. Blend until smooth.

Heat griddle or skillet; brush with oil. Spoon 1/4 cup batter at a time, spreading into a circle about 4 inches in diameter. Cook over medium heat until brown on bottom and dry on top. Sprinkle with grated cheese, if desired. Remove from griddle. Serve warm.

MAKES 5 THIN 4-INCH ROUNDS.

Stuffed Brussels Sprouts

A rare combination—good nutrition and excellent taste!

1 1/2 to 2 pounds Brussels sprouts
1/8 teaspoon salt
1 cup Italian salad dressing
1/2 cup cottage cheese, drained

1 (2-oz.) package blue cheese, crumbled
1/2 teaspoon grated onion
1/2 teaspoon seasoned salt

Combine Brussels sprouts, salt and enough water to cover Brussels sprouts in a medium saucepan. Cook over medium heat until crisp-tender, about 15 minutes; drain.

With a small melon baller or knife, remove center core from each cooked Brussels sprout. Reserve centers for another use. Place shells, cut side down, on paper towels to drain thoroughly, about 15 minutes.

Place drained Brussels sprouts in a medium bowl; pour salad dressing evenly over each Brussels sprout. Cover and refrigerate 6 hours or overnight; drain.

Combine cottage cheese, blue cheese, grated onion and seasoned salt in a small bowl. Spoon cheese mixture evenly into drained sprouts and arrange on a platter.

MAKES ABOUT 40 APPETIZERS.

Spiced Carrot Sticks

For variety, cut the carrots into thin round slices.

5 large carrots (about 1 pound)
1 cup white-wine vinegar
1/2 cup fresh orange juice

1/4 cup honey
1 tablespoon pickling spices

Peel carrots; cut into thin sticks. Combine vinegar, orange juice, honey and pickling spices in a nonaluminum saucepan. Add carrot sticks and bring to a boil over medium heat. Simmer over medium-low heat 8 to 10 minutes or until carrots are crisp-tender.

Remove pan from heat and cool on a wire rack 15 minutes. Pour carrots and marinade into a medium bowl. Cover tightly and refrigerate 6 hours or overnight. Drain and serve.

MAKES 8 TO 10 APPETIZER SERVINGS.

Stuffed Cucumber Slices

These are especially attractive on a Christmas appetizer tray.

1 large cucumber
4 ounces cream cheese, at room temperature
2 tablespoons crumbled blue cheese
1 teaspoon grated onion
2 teaspoons minced fresh parsley
1 teaspoon dried dill weed
30 to 36 pimiento strips

Score cucumber by pressing tines of a fork about 1/16 inch into peel at one end and pulling tines lengthwise, leaving grooves. Turn cucumber and continue scoring until entirely covered with lengthwise grooves. Trim ends; cut cucumber in half lengthwise. Use a spoon to scoop seeds from inside cucumber and discard seeds. Let cucumber halves drain, cut side down, on paper towels about 10 minutes.

Combine cream cheese, blue cheese, onion, parsley and dill weed in a small bowl. Spoon mixture into hollowed-out cucumber. Slice crosswise into 1/2-inch-wide slices. Garnish slices with pimiento strips. Serve immediately.

MAKES 30 TO 36 SLICES.

Greek-Style Mushrooms

Fennel seeds give the mushrooms a very subtle licorice flavor.

1 pound small mushrooms
1/2 cup olive oil or vegetable oil
1/4 cup dry white wine
2 tablespoons fresh lemon juice
1/2 cup water
1 clove garlic, crushed

1 teaspoon salt
1/4 teaspoon pepper
1 teaspoon sugar
1/4 teaspoon fennel seeds
1/2 teaspoon ground coriander

Wipe mushrooms with a damp cloth. Set aside in a large heatproof bowl. Combine remaining ingredients in a small saucepan. Bring to boil over medium heat; reduce heat and simmer about 2 minutes. Immediately, pour hot mixture over mushrooms. Cover and cool to room temperature. Refrigerate 6 hours or overnight. Drain and serve with wooden picks.

MAKES 65 TO 70 APPETIZERS.

Sausage-Stuffed Mushrooms

Save mushroom stems to enhance a salad, stew or soup.

8 ounces bulk pork sausage
2 tablespoons finely chopped onion
1 tablespoon finely chopped fresh parsley
1/8 teaspoon salt
1/8 teaspoon pepper
1 egg, beaten slightly
1/2 cup soft bread crumbs
16 to 18 large (1 1/2- to 1 3/4-inch) mushrooms
2 tablespoons freshly grated Parmesan cheese

Preheat oven to 350F (175C). Cook sausage and onion in a small skillet over medium heat, stirring to break up sausage, about 10 minutes. Remove from heat; drain well. Stir in parsley, salt, pepper, egg and bread crumbs.

Remove stems from mushrooms; use for another purpose. Spoon sausage mixture into mushroom caps, mounding each slightly. Place stuffed mushrooms in a shallow baking pan. Sprinkle with Parmesan cheese. Bake 8 to 10 minutes or until cheese browns slightly. Serve hot.

MAKES 16 TO 18 STUFFED MUSHROOMS.

Stuffed Snow Peas

An excellent make-ahead way to use leftover baked ham. Fill pea pods and refrigerate until serving time.

About 8 ounces fresh snow peas
2 cups finely chopped cooked ham
2 tablespoons fruit chutney, fruit finely chopped
2 tablespoons Dijon mustard
2 teaspoons prepared horseradish
1/2 cup low-calorie mayonnaise

Trim ends from pea pods. Bring about 4 cups lightly salted water to a boil in a medium saucepan. Add pea pods and simmer about 1 or 2 minutes or until crisp-tender; drain. Rinse in cold water; drain and refrigerate until chilled.

Combine ham, chutney, mustard, horseradish and mayonnaise in a small bowl. Carefully slit 1 side of each pea pod. Use a small spoon to fill each pod with ham mixture. Arrange on flat platter or tray, with pea pods touching to keep them upright. Cover and refrigerate at least 1 hour.

MAKES 50 TO 55.

Parmesan- and Goat-Cheese Potato Wedges

A new twist to the classic baked potato with cheese. It's slightly messy to pick up with your fingers—but well worth the effort.

2 1/4 ounces (about 3/4 cup) freshly grated Parmesan cheese
1 1/3 ounces (about 1/3 cup) crumbled goat cheese
3 tablespoons finely chopped green onion
1/2 teaspoon salt
1/4 teaspoon pepper
2 tablespoons finely chopped fresh parsley
4 large baking potatoes, scrubbed
1/4 cup margarine or butter, melted

Preheat oven to 400F (205C). Combine Parmesan cheese, goat cheese, green onion, salt, pepper and parsley in a small bowl.

Cut each unpeeled potato lengthwise into 6 wedges. Brush cut sides of potato wedges with margarine or butter. Gently press cheese mixture over potatoes. Place potatoes, skin side down, in a 10 × 15-inch baking pan. Bake 20 to 25 minutes or until potatoes are tender. Serve warm.

MAKES 24 WEDGES.

Hot Potato Nests

Create a new favorite potato dish with a horseradish-flavored filling.

3 potatoes (about 5 to 6 ounces each)	2 teaspoons prepared horseradish
2 tablespoons freshly grated Parmesan cheese	1/4 cup sour cream
	2 green onions, finely chopped
1 ounce (1/4 cup) Monterey Jack cheese, shredded	1/2 teaspoon salt
	1/8 teaspoon pepper

Place potatoes in a medium saucepan and cover with water. Cook until soft but not falling apart, about 20 minutes. Drain and chill.

Preheat oven to 425F (220C). Lightly butter sides and bottoms of 7 muffin cups. Peel and coarsely shred cold cooked potatoes. Gently press about 1/3 cup potato shreds against bottom and side of each muffin cup. Sprinkle with Parmesan and Jack cheeses.

Bake about 30 minutes or until lightly browned. Combine horseradish, sour cream, green onions, salt and pepper in a small bowl. Spoon mixture into center of hot potatoes.

MAKES 7 NESTS.

Double-Squash Cups

An interesting change from the traditional vegetable dish.

2 tablespoons margarine or butter	1/2 teaspoon salt
1 small leek, thinly sliced	1/8 teaspoon pepper
1 clove garlic, crushed	1/4 cup all-purpose flour
1 medium zucchini, shredded	1/2 cup milk
1 medium yellow pattypan squash, shredded	2 ounces (1/2 cup) sharp Cheddar cheese, shredded
3 eggs, beaten slightly	

Preheat oven to 325F (165C). Grease 12 (2 1/2-inch) muffin cups. Melt margarine or butter in a 10-inch skillet over medium heat. Add leek and garlic and cook, stirring, 5 minutes or until leek is soft. Add zucchini and pattypan squash and cook 3 minutes. Remove from heat.

Combine eggs, salt, pepper, flour and milk in a medium bowl. Stir in zucchini mixture. Spoon into prepared muffin cups. Sprinkle with shredded cheese. Bake 18 to 20 minutes or until set. Cool 5 minutes; remove from pan.

MAKES 12.

Stuffed Radish Roses

These hors d'oeuvres are as pretty as they are tasty.

2 bunches (20 to 25) radishes
1 (3-oz.) package cream cheese,
  at room temperature
2 tablespoons crumbled blue cheese

1/8 teaspoon salt
1 tablespoon milk
1 tablespoon minced fresh parsley

Cut stems and roots from radishes. Make deep X-cuts from top of radishes almost to bottoms. Let radishes stand in iced water in the refrigerator 2 to 3 hours to open.

Combine cream cheese, blue cheese, salt, milk and parsley in a small bowl. Drain radishes; pat dry with paper towels. Spoon cheese mixture into center and on top of each radish.

MAKES 20 TO 25 APPETIZER SERVINGS.

Spinach-Filled Filo Cups

We prefer to eat the spinach cups while they're hot from the oven, but they're still good at room temperature.

1 (10-oz.) package frozen chopped spinach, thawed
10 medium mushrooms, chopped
6 ounces (3/4 cup) ricotta cheese, drained
3 tablespoons pine nuts, chopped
1/8 teaspoon ground nutmeg
1 egg, beaten slightly
1/2 teaspoon seasoned salt
4 tablespoons freshly grated Parmesan cheese
4 sheets filo dough
6 tablespoons margarine or butter, melted

Preheat oven to 375F (190C). Drain spinach in a strainer, using the back of a spoon to press out excess liquid. Combine drained spinach, mushrooms, ricotta cheese, pine nuts, nutmeg, egg, seasoned salt and 2 tablespoons of the Parmesan cheese; set aside.

Brush each sheet of filo with melted margarine or butter; stack filo sheets. Cut filo crosswise into fourths and lengthwise into thirds to form 12 (4-layer) squares. Gently press each square into a 2 1/2-inch muffin cup or a 6-ounce custard cup.

Spoon 1/4 cup spinach mixture into each filo-lined cup. Sprinkle with remaining 2 tablespoons Parmesan cheese. Bake 25 minutes or until golden brown and filling is set. Remove from oven; let stand 5 minutes. Remove from cups.

MAKES 12 SERVINGS.

Pesto-Stuffed Cherry Tomatoes

The green of the filling and red of the tomatoes make a colorful and appetizing addition to a tray of fresh vegetables, or an interesting contrast of flavors when served with grilled chicken.

1/2 cup lightly packed fresh basil leaves
1/4 cup lightly packed fresh parsley leaves
1/4 cup (about 1 ounce) freshly grated Parmesan cheese
1/4 teaspoon salt
1/8 teaspoon pepper
2 tablespoons olive oil
1 clove garlic, coarsely chopped
4 ounces (1/2 cup) ricotta cheese, drained
20 cherry tomatoes

Combine basil, parsley, Parmesan cheese, salt, pepper, olive oil and garlic in a blender or food processor fitted with metal blade. Process until finely chopped. Stir in ricotta cheese.

Make an X-cut in bottom of each tomato almost to stem end. Carefully open tomato, being careful not to tear it, and scoop out pulp and seeds. Spoon or pipe about 2 teaspoons of mixture into each tomato.

MAKES 20 STUFFED TOMATOES.

Little Savory Bites

Salmon-Stuffed Tomatoes

Decorate your appetizer tray with these colorful bite-size morsels.

25 to 30 cherry tomatoes
1 (3-oz.) package thinly sliced smoked salmon (lox)
1 (3-oz.) package cream cheese, at room temperature
1 teaspoon fresh lemon juice
1 tablespoon minced watercress leaves
Salt and pepper, to taste
Watercress sprigs, for garnish

Cut a thin slice from stem end of each tomato; scoop pulp and seeds from center with a small sharp-edged spoon, or make a deep X-cut from top of tomato almost to bottom. Carefully open tomato at top and scoop out pulp and seeds. Place tomatoes cut side down on paper towels to drain.

Chop salmon until very fine. Stir cream cheese in a small bowl until smooth. Stir in chopped salmon, lemon juice and 1 tablespoon minced watercress.

Sprinkle inside of drained cherry tomatoes with salt and pepper to taste. Fill each with salmon mixture; top each with a small sprig of watercress.

MAKES 25 TO 30 APPETIZERS.

Cheese-Stuffed Zucchini

Zucchini is easier to stuff when it is slightly undercooked and the texture is better.

4 small zucchini (about 3 ounces each)
1 tablespoon margarine or butter, melted
2 ounces (1/2 cup) Swiss cheese, shredded
1/2 cup soft bread crumbs

1/4 teaspoon salt
1/8 teaspoon pepper
1 teaspoon finely chopped fresh marjoram leaves
2 tablespoons freshly grated Parmesan cheese

Place zucchini in a medium saucepan with a tight-fitting lid and add enough water to cover zucchini. Cook, covered, over medium heat 9 to 10 minutes or until barely tender. Trim ends; cut in half lengthwise. Use a spoon to scoop out pulp, leaving 1/4-inch-thick shells. Do not puncture outer shell; set aside. Chop zucchini pulp until very fine.

Preheat oven to 375F (190C). Grease a 7 × 11-inch baking pan. Combine zucchini pulp, margarine or butter, Swiss cheese, bread crumbs, salt, pepper and marjoram.

Spoon mixture evenly into zucchini shells. Sprinkle evenly with Parmesan cheese. Arrange zucchini in greased pan. Bake 10 to 15 minutes or until hot. Cut each stuffed zucchini half into 4 to 6 diagonal slices. Serve warm.

MAKES 32 TO 48 APPETIZERS.

Zucchini Appetizer Pie

Serve this popular dish as part of your next brunch or appetizer buffet.

4 medium zucchini
2 tablespoons vegetable oil
2 eggs
1 cup cottage cheese, drained
1/4 cup margarine or butter, at room temperature
1/4 cup all-purpose flour
1/2 teaspoon baking powder
1/4 teaspoon salt
1 cup sour cream
1/4 cup (about 1 ounce) freshly grated Parmesan cheese
1 tomato, peeled and thinly sliced
Parsley sprigs, for garnish

Cut zucchini crosswise into 1/4-inch-thick slices. Heat oil in large skillet over medium heat. Add zucchini; sauté until softened but not mushy, about 3 minutes. Line bottom and side of a 9-inch pie plate with sautéed zucchini slices; set aside.

Preheat oven to 350F (175C). Beat eggs in a large bowl. Beat in cottage cheese and margarine or butter until almost smooth. Stir in flour, baking powder and salt until blended; then stir in sour cream and Parmesan cheese. Pour evenly into zucchini-lined pie plate. Gently smooth top with spatula. Carefully arrange tomato slices over top of filling.

Bake 35 to 45 minutes or until firm in center. Cool on a rack 10 minutes. Invert onto a 12-inch-round platter. Garnish center with parsley sprigs. Cut into small wedges; serve warm.

MAKES 16 TO 20 WEDGES.

Zucchini Bites

For better color, flavor, and nutrition, shred the zucchini with the peel on. Plain or chile-flavored Monterey Jack cheese can also be used.

2 eggs
2 medium zucchini, shredded
1 tablespoon grated onion
1 tablespoon chopped fresh parsley
1/2 teaspoon salt
1/8 teaspoon pepper
1/4 cup fine dry bread crumbs
2 tablespoons margarine or butter, melted
4 ounces (1 cup) pesto-flavored Monterey Jack cheese, shredded

Preheat oven to 350F (175C). Grease an 8-inch-square pan; set aside. Beat eggs in a medium bowl; stir in zucchini, onion, parsley, salt, pepper, bread crumbs, margarine or butter and half of the cheese. Spoon evenly into prepared pan; sprinkle with remaining cheese.

Bake 20 to 25 minutes or until set. Use a sharp knife to cut 7 rows vertically and 7 rows horizontally making 3/4-inch squares; serve warm.

MAKES 49 SQUARES.

Little Savory Bites

Small Meals

Small meals fit our more relaxed, casual lifestyle and the differing schedules of various family members. These recipes, some of which are for one-dish meals, are easy to do and can be served for brunches, lunches, suppers and casual dinners.

Ingredients are all available at a well-stocked supermarket even though many of the dishes offer tastes of exotic places. There are also more familiar favorites that have been made easier without sacrificing flavor.

Herb-Grilled Chicken

A light marinade makes this a welcome change from traditional barbecued chicken. Fresh herbs combined with mustard, lemon juice and wine bring out the best in the chicken.

3 pounds frying-chicken pieces
1/4 cup vegetable oil
2 tablespoons fresh lemon juice
2 tablespoons dry white wine
1 tablespoon finely chopped fresh rosemary

1 teaspoon finely chopped fresh thyme
2 tablespoons sweet-hot mustard
1 teaspoon salt
1/4 teaspoon pepper

Arrange chicken pieces in a single layer in a large, shallow nonaluminum baking dish. Combine oil, lemon juice, wine, rosemary, thyme, mustard, salt and pepper in a small bowl; pour mixture over chicken. Cover and refrigerate at least 4 hours or overnight, turning chicken pieces once. Remove chicken from marinade; set marinade aside.

Preheat grill. Place chicken on grill rack about 4 inches from heat. Grill chicken, turning frequently and brushing with reserved marinade several times during cooking. Cook chicken a total of 30 to 40 minutes or until juices run clear when pierced with a fork.

MAKES 4 OR 5 SERVINGS.

Chicken Siam

You can either bake or broil the chicken. Baking results in a moister chicken; broiling makes the chicken crunchier.

6 boneless, skinless chicken breast halves (about 1 1/2 pounds)
1 tablespoon margarine or butter, melted
1 tablespoon vegetable oil
1/2 cup peanuts
1/3 cup chutney
1 tablespoon fresh lemon juice
1 jalapeño chile, seeded and chopped
1/2 teaspoon salt
1/2 cup half and half

Preheat oven to 350F (175C). Cut chicken breasts lengthwise into 4 or 5 long strips; thread each strip onto a 6-inch skewer. Arrange skewered chicken in a large shallow baking pan.

Combine margarine or butter and oil in a small bowl; brush on chicken. Combine peanuts, chutney, lemon juice, jalapeño chile, salt, and half and half in a blender or food processor. Process until finely chopped, but not pureed. Brush top of chicken with peanut sauce.

Bake chicken 7 minutes. Turn chicken and brush other side with sauce. Return to oven; bake 3 minutes or until center of chicken is no longer pink. Serve warm.

MAKES 24 TO 30 KABOBS.

VARIATION

If you prefer broiled chicken, brush skewered chicken with sauce. Broil 4 to 5 inches from heat source 3 minutes. Turn and brush with sauce. Broil 2 minutes or until chicken is no longer pink in center.

Barbecued Chicken 'n' Noodles

Using the marinade as a sauce for the noodles and grilling boneless chicken parts make this traditional recipe with a modern twist especially easy.

1/4 cup soy sauce
3 tablespoons honey
3/4 cup chili sauce
2 tablespoons prepared mustard
1 clove garlic, crushed
2 tablespoons fresh lemon juice
1/4 teaspoon salt

1/8 teaspoon pepper
4 boneless, skinless chicken thighs (about 1 1/2 pounds)
7 to 8 ounces thin noodles
4 teaspoons cornstarch
2 green onions, thinly sliced

Combine soy sauce, honey, chili sauce, mustard, garlic, lemon juice, salt and pepper in a medium nonaluminum bowl. Add chicken, turning to coat both sides; cover and refrigerate at least 4 hours or overnight.

Preheat grill or broiler. Broil or grill about 4 to 5 inches from heat about 6 minutes. Brush chicken with marinade; turn and cook 4 to 5 minutes or until no longer pink in center. Cut chicken into thin strips.

Meanwhile, cook noodles; drain. Stir cornstarch into remaining marinade. Bring to a boil; cook, stirring, 1 minute or until thickened. Spoon chicken strips over cooked noodles. Top with sauce and green onions. Toss until combined.

MAKES 5 OR 6 SERVINGS.

Shangri-La Drumsticks

To prepare these exotic drumsticks for a picnic, cook them at least four hours before serving time. Thoroughly chill them in the refrigerator and keep them cold en route to the picnic.

1/2 cup plain yogurt
1/2 teaspoon curry powder
1/4 teaspoon ground cumin
1 clove garlic, crushed
1 tablespoon fresh lemon juice
1/4 teaspoon salt

1/8 teaspoon ground red pepper
1/2 cup fine dry bread crumbs
2 tablespoons sesame seeds
1 tablespoon margarine or butter, melted
8 or 9 chicken drumsticks

Preheat oven to 375F (190C). Combine yogurt, curry powder, cumin, garlic, lemon juice, salt and red pepper in a shallow bowl. Combine bread crumbs and sesame seeds in another shallow bowl. Pour melted margarine or butter into a shallow baking pan. Dip chicken drumsticks into yogurt mixture, then into bread-crumb mixture.

Place coated chicken in buttered pan. Bake 30 minutes. Turn drumsticks over and return to oven. Bake 20 minutes or until golden brown. Serve warm or refrigerate until serving time.

MAKES 8 OR 9 DRUMSTICKS.

Small Meals

Curried Chicken in Pasta Shells

Finely chop the pieces of fruit in the chutney before adding them to the dressing.

12 jumbo pasta shells
1/2 cup plain yogurt
1/4 cup mayonnaise
2 teaspoons curry powder
1 teaspoon fresh lemon juice
2 tablespoons chutney

1/4 cup shredded sweetened coconut
1/4 teaspoon salt
1/8 teaspoon pepper
2 cups chopped cooked chicken
2 tablespoons chopped peanuts

Cook pasta shells in boiling salted water according to package directions; drain.

While pasta cooks, combine yogurt, mayonnaise, curry powder, lemon juice, chutney, coconut, salt, pepper, and chicken in a medium bowl. Spoon into drained pasta shells. Sprinkle with peanuts. Serve warm or cover, refrigerate and serve cold.

MAKES 12 SHELLS.

Maple Orange Chicken

American maple syrup is accented with Asian flavors of ginger and soy sauce.

1/4 cup maple syrup
3 tablespoons vegetable oil
2 tablespoons soy sauce
1 teaspoon grated orange peel
2 teaspoons grated peeled gingerroot

1 clove garlic, crushed
8 chicken thighs or chicken breast halves
2 tablespoons sesame seeds

Combine maple syrup, oil, soy sauce, orange peel, ginger and garlic in a medium bowl. Add chicken and stir to coat. Cover and refrigerate several hours or overnight.

Preheat oven to 375F (190C). Arrange a single layer of chicken in a shallow baking pan; brush tops with marinade. Bake about 20 minutes. Reduce heat to 325F (165C). Turn chicken over and brush with marinade. Sprinkle chicken with sesame seeds. Bake 25 minutes or until juices run clear when chicken is pierced in center.

MAKES 8 PIECES.

VARIATION

Cut cooked chicken into bite-size pieces and serve with wooden picks as an appetizer at your next party.

Chicken and Prosciutto Roulades

Serve whole roulades as a main dish or cut each into four crosswise slices for appetizers.

8 boneless, skinless chicken breast halves
1 clove garlic, crushed
3 ounces thinly sliced prosciutto, coarsely chopped
1/4 cup sun-dried tomatoes (oil packed), chopped
2 green onions, chopped
1 tablespoon chopped fresh basil
1/3 cup ricotta cheese, drained
2 tablespoons margarine or butter, melted
1/2 cup seasoned dry bread crumbs
2 tablespoons vegetable oil
1 (14 1/2-oz.) can low-sodium chicken broth
4 teaspoons cornstarch
1 tablespoon cold water

Place each chicken breast between waxed paper or plastic wrap. Lightly pound with a wooden mallet; turn and pound other side until about 1/2 inch thick. Set aside.

Combine garlic, prosciutto, sun-dried tomatoes, onions, basil and ricotta cheese in a medium bowl. Spread cheese mixture on each pounded chicken breast. Roll up chicken to enclose filling; secure with small metal skewers. Roll in margarine or butter; then bread crumbs.

Heat oil in a 12-inch skillet over medium-high heat. Add chicken and cook, turning, until browned. Add broth, cover, and cook over medium heat about 15 minutes or until chicken is cooked through.

Remove chicken and keep warm. Combine cornstarch and water. Stir into broth in skillet. Bring to a boil, stirring constantly. Simmer 1 minute or until thickened. Slice each chicken roll into 4 pieces or serve whole. Serve with sauce.

MAKES 8 MAIN-DISH SERVINGS OR 32 APPETIZERS.

Giant Chicken-Stuffed Shells

A great main dish at outdoor get-togethers, these shells are filled with the flavors of sun-dried tomatoes and chicken.

10 to 12 giant pasta shells
1/4 cup sour cream
1/4 cup mayonnaise
1 tablespoon finely chopped green onion
1 teaspoon prepared mustard
1 hard-cooked egg, chopped
2 tablespoons chopped sun-dried tomatoes (oil packed)
1/4 teaspoon salt
1/8 teaspoon pepper
1 cup diced cooked chicken
2 ounces (about 1/2 cup) mozzarella cheese, diced
2 tablespoons pine nuts or pistachios

Bring 3 quarts salted water to a boil in a 4-quart saucepan over high heat. Add pasta shells; bring to a boil and cook 8 to 10 minutes or until barely tender. Immediately cover with cold water; drain well.

Combine sour cream, mayonnaise, green onion, mustard, egg, sun-dried tomatoes, salt and pepper in a medium bowl. Stir in chicken and cheese. Spoon into cooked shells. Sprinkle pine nuts or pistachios on top. Serve immediately, or cover and refrigerate up to 24 hours.

MAKES 10 TO 12 SHELLS.

Chicken and Water Chestnuts

Slightly undercook the red bell pepper and water chestnuts for color and crunch.

2 tablespoons vegetable oil
1 clove garlic, crushed
5 or 6 chicken breast halves, skinned
1 cup chicken broth or bouillon
3 tablespoons cornstarch
1/4 cup soy sauce
1/4 cup white wine

1/4 teaspoon salt
1/8 teaspoon pepper
1 red bell pepper, cut into 1-inch chunks
1 (8-oz.) can sliced water chestnuts, drained
Cooked rice, to serve

In a 10- or 12-inch skillet, heat oil and garlic over medium heat. Add chicken breasts; cook about 10 minutes or until browned. Turn and brown other side. Combine chicken broth and cornstarch in a small bowl; stir until smooth. Add to chicken in skillet along with soy sauce, wine, salt and pepper. Simmer, stirring, until thickened and bubbly. Stir in bell pepper and water chestnuts; cook and stir over medium heat 1 or 2 minutes. Serve with rice.

MAKES 5 OR 6 SERVINGS.

Chicken-Mustard Rolls

Leave each roll-up whole for a traditional-size serving or cut each into three or four pieces for appetizer servings.

4 boneless, skinless chicken breast halves (about 1 lb.)
8 small green onions
Salt and freshly ground pepper
1/4 cup margarine or butter, melted
2 teaspoons sweet and spicy mustard
1 teaspoon Worcestershire sauce
1 cup soft bread crumbs

Preheat oven to 350F (175C). Lightly pound chicken breasts between waxed paper to about 1/4-inch thickness. Cut each chicken breast in half lengthwise. Place 1 green onion lengthwise on each chicken piece. Sprinkle with salt and pepper. Roll up each chicken piece, securing with a small wooden pick, if necessary.

Combine melted margarine or butter, mustard and Worcestershire sauce in a small bowl. Dip each chicken roll in margarine mixture, then roll in bread crumbs. Place in a shallow baking pan. Bake 17 to 20 minutes or until juices run clear when chicken is pierced with a fork. Serve hot.

MAKES 8 SERVINGS.

Almond-Cherry Turkey Cutlets

The bing cherry flavor blends with the red wine to create an exciting sauce for the turkey.

3/4 cup dried bing cherries
1/4 cup honey
2 cups red wine
1/4 teaspoon almond extract
1 tablespoon cornstarch
2 tablespoons fresh orange juice
2 tablespoons margarine or butter
1/3 cup all-purpose flour

1/4 teaspoon salt
1/8 teaspoon pepper
5 or 6 raw turkey cutlets or breast slices
2 to 3 tablespoons slivered almonds, toasted (see Note, page 205), for garnish
Cooked rice, to serve

Combine cherries, honey, wine and almond extract in a medium saucepan over medium heat. Bring to a boil; simmer uncovered about 20 minutes or until cherries are plump and liquid is reduced. Stir together cornstarch and orange juice in a small bowl. Add to wine mixture; bring to a boil. Simmer, stirring, 1 minute; remove from heat.

Heat margarine or butter in a large skillet over medium-high heat. Combine flour, salt and pepper in a shallow bowl. Dip both sides of cutlets in flour mixture. Add cutlets, in batches, to hot margarine or butter and sauté until browned, about 1 1/2 to 2 minutes. Turn and cook other side. Repeat cooking remaining cutlets.

To serve, spoon cherries and sauce over each cutlet. Sprinkle with almonds. Serve with rice.

MAKES 5 OR 6 SERVINGS.

Orange and Cranberry Turkey Loaf

It's quick and easy to prepare—just combine all ingredients and bake!

1 pound ground turkey
1 egg, beaten slightly
1 small onion, finely chopped
1 stalk celery, finely chopped
3/4 cup soft bread crumbs
1/2 teaspoon salt

1/4 teaspoon pepper
1 teaspoon grated orange peel
1/2 cup jellied cranberry sauce
2 tablespoons fresh orange juice
1/8 teaspoon ground nutmeg

Preheat oven to 350F (175C). Grease an 8- or 9-inch-round baking dish. Combine all ingredients in a large bowl. Press into greased dish. Bake 45 to 55 minutes or until cooked through. Cool in pan 10 minutes. Turn out of pan and cut into slices. Serve warm or chilled.

MAKES ABOUT 6 SERVINGS.

Stuffed Turkey Roll-ups with Red Wine Sauce

These roll-ups are an appealing change of pace from the usual turkey dish. Water chestnuts add a nice crunch and using a package of stuffing mix makes it easy.

6 or 7 turkey cutlets (about 3 ounces each)
1 (6-oz.) package stuffing mix (1 3/4 cups)
1 tablespoon minced green onion
1/4 cup finely chopped water chestnuts
1/3 cup orange juice
2 tablespoons margarine or butter, melted

RED WINE SAUCE

2 tablespoons cornstarch
1/2 cup chicken broth or bouillon
1/3 cup red currant jelly
1 clove garlic, crushed
1/4 cup red wine

Preheat oven to 350F (175C). Grease a shallow baking pan. Lightly pound each cutlet with a wooden mallet to about 1/4-inch thickness. Combine stuffing mix, green onion, water chestnuts and orange juice in a medium bowl. Spread each turkey cutlet with stuffing mixture. Roll up to enclose stuffing; secure with wooden picks. Place in greased baking pan.

Brush turkey with margarine or butter. Cover with foil. Bake 30 to 40 minutes or until cooked through.

While turkey is cooking, prepare sauce. Spoon warm sauce over each serving.

MAKES 6 OR 7 SERVINGS.

RED WINE SAUCE

Dissolve cornstarch in chicken broth or bouillon in a small saucepan. Stir in currant jelly, garlic and red wine. Cook, stirring, over medium heat until thickened and translucent.

Orange Risotto with Turkey

Arborio rice contributes an exciting new flavor combination to leftover roasted turkey.

1/4 cup margarine or butter
1 small onion, chopped
1/2 cup chopped mushrooms
1 cup diced cooked turkey
1/2 cup uncooked Arborio rice
3 cups chicken broth or stock

1/2 cup fresh orange juice
1/2 teaspoon grated orange peel
1/4 teaspoon salt
1/8 teaspoon pepper
Cranberry sauce (optional)

Combine margarine or butter and onion in a 10-inch skillet over medium heat. Cook, stirring occasionally, until onion is soft but not browned. Add mushrooms, cooked turkey and rice.

Heat broth and orange juice to the boiling point. Add 1/2 cup hot broth mixture to rice mixture. Cook, stirring, until broth is absorbed. Continue cooking and stirring constantly while adding hot broth mixture, 1/2 cup at a time, until rice is creamy and grains are slightly firm in center, about 20 minutes.

Stir in grated orange peel, salt and pepper. Serve with cranberry sauce, if desired.

MAKES ABOUT 4 SERVINGS.

Small Meals

Pinto Bean and Turkey Chili

Corn or tortilla chips are at their best when crushed with your hands into pieces about 1 inch in diameter.

1 pound dried pinto beans, soaked overnight
10 cups water
8 ounces turkey sausage
1 medium onion, chopped
1 clove garlic, crushed
1 jalapeño chile, seeded and chopped
1 tablespoon chili powder
1 teaspoon ground cumin
1 teaspoon salt
2 (8-oz.) cans tomato sauce
3 ounces (3/4 cup) Monterey Jack cheese, shredded, to serve
2 cups crushed corn or tortilla chips, to serve
2 cups shredded cabbage, to serve
3 radishes, sliced, to serve

Drain beans and pour into a large pan. Add enough water to cover and cook beans, uncovered, about 2 hours or until tender. Drain beans, reserving liquid.

Cook sausage, onion, garlic and jalapeño chile in a 10-inch skillet over medium heat, stirring to break up sausage, until sausage is browned, about 10 minutes.

Stir in chili powder, cumin, salt, tomato sauce and 1/2 cup of reserved bean liquid. Stir in cooked beans. Heat until bubbly. Spoon into large soup bowls. Top with cheese, chips, cabbage and radishes.

MAKES ABOUT 6 SERVINGS.

Turkey Tortilla Crisp

A very special way to dress up leftover turkey.

1 (14- to 15-oz.) can cannellini or pinto beans, drained and rinsed
1 jalapeño chile, seeded and finely chopped
2 green onions, chopped
2 tablespoons chopped fresh cilantro
1/4 cup plain yogurt, plus extra to serve
1/3 cup vegetable oil
4 (8-inch) flour tortillas
1 large tomato, chopped
2 cups smoked cooked turkey
1 avocado, peeled and sliced

Combine drained beans, jalapeño chile, green onions, cilantro and 1/4 cup yogurt in a medium bowl.

Heat oil in a large skillet over medium-high heat. Add 1 tortilla at a time and cook on both sides until crisp. Drain on paper towels. Spoon 1/4 of bean mixture on each crisp tortilla. Top each tortilla with chopped tomato, turkey and avocado, then yogurt.

MAKES 4 SERVINGS.

Broiled Halibut with Tropical Salsa

A perfect dish for a busy day: make the salsa the night before and refrigerate it to allow flavors to blend.

1 mango, peeled, pitted and chopped
1 kiwi fruit, peeled and chopped
1 small red bell pepper, chopped
1 jalapeño chile, seeded and finely chopped
1/2 cup chopped fresh cilantro
4 tablespoons vegetable oil
2 tablespoons fresh lime juice
5 or 6 halibut steaks (about 1 inch thick)
Salt and pepper

Combine mango, kiwi, pepper, chile, cilantro, 2 tablespoons of the oil and the lime juice in a medium bowl. Cover and refrigerate several hours or overnight.

Heat grill or broiler. Brush halibut with 1 tablespoon of the oil. Grill or broil 4 to 5 inches from heat 5 or 6 minutes. Turn steaks, brush with remaining tablespoon of oil and cook another 5 or 6 minutes. Sprinkle with salt and pepper. Serve with salsa.

MAKES 5 OR 6 SERVINGS.

Hearty Salmon Chowder

This filling chowder makes a popular and satisfying main dish for a cold winter evening.

8 to 10 ounces salmon fillet or sole fillet
2 cups chicken bouillon or broth
3 slices bacon, diced
1 medium potato, peeled and diced
2 leeks, thinly sliced
3 tablespoons cornstarch
3 cups milk
2 tablespoons dry white wine
2 green onions, thinly sliced

Remove skin from salmon. Combine salmon and broth in a saucepan. Bring to a boil; simmer about 7 minutes or until salmon begins to flake. Remove salmon; save broth. Cut salmon into small pieces; set aside.

Cook bacon in a large skillet over medium heat; drain off fat. Add potato, leeks and reserved broth. Cook about 15 minutes or until potato is tender. Dissolve cornstarch in milk; add to skillet. Cook, stirring, until bubbly and slightly thickened. Stir in cooked salmon and wine. Top with green onions.

MAKES 6 CUPS.

Dilled Smoked Salmon Tarts

Impressive little pastry cups, chock-full of salmon with accents of dill.

1 recipe Rich Pastry (page 174)
3 eggs
1/2 cup milk
1 tablespoon fresh lemon juice
1 tablespoon chopped chives

4 medium mushrooms, coarsely chopped
1 (3-oz.) package thinly sliced smoked salmon (lox), chopped
1 tablespoon chopped fresh dill

Preheat oven to 375F (190C). Roll out pastry to about a 16 × 8-inch rectangle. Cut into 8 (4-inch) squares. Fit into 8 (6-oz.) custard cups.

Beat eggs. Combine milk, lemon juice, chives, mushrooms, smoked salmon and dill in a medium bowl. Spoon mixture into pastry-lined cups. Bake about 25 minutes or until centers are firm.

MAKES 8 TARTS.

Grilled Ginger-Honey Shrimp

The slightly spicy sauce for the shrimp has a teriyaki base flavored with a combination of favorite international ingredients.

1 tablespoon grated gingerroot	2 tablespoons vegetable oil
1 tablespoon fresh lemon juice	1/4 teaspoon chili oil
1 clove garlic, crushed	25 to 30 medium raw shrimp, peeled and deveined
2 tablespoons honey	
1/2 cup teriyaki sauce	Cooked rice, to serve

Combine ginger, lemon juice, garlic, honey, teriyaki sauce, vegetable oil and chili oil in a small bowl. Thread 5 or 6 shrimp onto each skewer. Place skewered shrimp in a shallow platter or pan. Brush with ginger mixture. Cover and refrigerate several hours or overnight.

Preheat broiler or grill. Broil shrimp about 2 minutes on each side, brushing several times with marinade. Serve with rice.

MAKES 5 OR 6 SERVINGS.

Spicy Chops with Mango Glaze

If boneless pork is not available, purchase pork chops and remove the bones.

5 or 6 (1/2-inch-thick) boneless pork chops or cutlets
1/4 teaspoon ground sage
1/4 teaspoon ground allspice
1/4 teaspoon ground cinnamon
1/4 teaspoon salt
1/8 teaspoon pepper
1 tablespoon vegetable oil
1 whole fresh mango, peeled, pitted and chopped
1/4 cup fruit chutney
2 tablespoons orange liqueur
1/4 cup chopped macadamia nuts or toasted coconut

Preheat oven to 375F (190C). Remove any excess fat from pork. Combine sage, allspice, cinnamon, salt and pepper in a small bowl. Brush both sides of pork with oil; then rub with spices. Let stand about 10 minutes.

Arrange pork in an ungreased baking pan. Bake 20 minutes.

Meanwhile, combine mango, chutney and liqueur in a blender or food processor. Blend until finely chopped. Remove 1/4 cup of mixture; refrigerate remaining mixture. Brush the 1/4 cup mango mixture on top of baked pork. Bake another 20 minutes or until tender. Sprinkle pork with macadamia nuts or coconut. Serve with remaining sauce.

MAKES 5 OR 6 SERVINGS.

South Seas Pork

Serve with a selection of cut-up tropical fruits to complete the island theme.

1/3 cup white wine
1/4 cup vegetable oil
1 tablespoon grated gingerroot
1 clove garlic, crushed
3 tablespoons soy sauce

2 tablespoons honey
1 (1 1/4- to 1 1/2-lb.) boneless pork tenderloin
2 teaspoons cornstarch

Combine wine, oil, ginger, garlic, soy sauce and honey in a small bowl. Pour over pork in a shallow dish or self-sealing plastic bag. Refrigerate 6 hours or overnight, rotating pork at least twice and brushing with marinade.

Preheat oven to 325F (165C). Place pork on a rack in a pan; reserve marinade. Roast pork about 1 hour or until thermometer inserted in center reads 160F (70C). Brush with marinade twice while roasting.

Pour drippings and any remaining marinade into a small saucepan. Stir in cornstarch. Cook, stirring, over medium-high heat until slightly thickened. Slice cooked pork. Serve with sauce.

MAKES 6 TO 8 SERVINGS.

Multicolored Pozole

For a colorful change, substitute this flavorful main dish for traditional chili.

1 pound lean boneless pork chops or shoulder
1 tablespoon vegetable oil
1 medium onion, chopped
1 medium red bell pepper, chopped
1 to 2 jalapeño chiles, seeded and finely chopped
1 teaspoon chili powder
1/2 teaspoon salt
1 cup chicken broth
1 (15-oz.) can white hominy, drained and rinsed
1 (15-oz.) can yellow hominy, drained and rinsed
1 tablespoon chopped fresh cilantro

Trim off any fat and cut pork into 1/2-inch cubes or strips. Heat oil in a 10-inch skillet. Add pork and onion and sauté until pork is lightly browned. Stir in bell pepper, jalapeño chile, chili powder, salt, broth and white and yellow hominy. Cover and simmer about 1 1/2 hours or until pork is tender. Serve in large soup bowls. Sprinkle with cilantro.

MAKES 4 TO 6 SERVINGS.

Glazed Orange Mustard Ham

A quick and easy glaze to glamorize a ham steak.

2 tablespoons Dijon mustard
3 tablespoons chili sauce
3 tablespoons pure maple syrup
2 tablespoons fresh orange juice
1 tablespoon vegetable oil
1 (1-lb.) fully cooked ham steak

Preheat broiler. Combine mustard, chili sauce, maple syrup, orange juice and vegetable oil in a small bowl.

Place ham on a baking sheet. Brush top of ham with mustard mixture. Broil 4 to 5 minutes; turn. Brush with mustard mixture and broil about 3 to 4 minutes or until browned. Cut into 4 equal pieces.

MAKES 4 SERVINGS.

Small Meals

Tortilla-Cheese Stack

Favorite Mexican food flavors that have been popular for generations are stacked together for a change of pace.

1/2 cup vegetable oil
6 (8-inch) flour tortillas
1 (15-oz.) can black refried beans
2 green onions, chopped
1 cup shredded jicama
1 medium tomato, chopped
1 (4-oz.) can diced green chiles, drained
4 ounces (1 cup) Fontina cheese, shredded
1/2 cup (1 1/2 oz.) freshly grated Parmesan cheese
1 tablespoon chopped fresh cilantro

Heat oil in a 9-inch skillet over medium-high heat. Add a tortilla and cook about 3 minutes per side until both sides are crispy and a light-golden color. Drain on paper towels. Repeat with remaining tortillas. Keep warm.

Preheat oven to 350F (175C). Place 2 cooked tortillas on a large baking sheet. Spread each with half of the refried beans; then with green onions. Top both with a second tortilla. Top both with jicama, tomatoes and chiles, then half of the Fontina cheese. Top each with a third tortilla. Sprinkle with remaining Fontina cheese and Parmesan cheese.

Bake 5 to 8 minutes or until cheese melts. Remove from oven. Sprinkle with cilantro. Cut each stack into 5 or 6 wedges. Serve immediately.

MAKES 10 TO 12 SERVINGS.

Roquefort Torta

Create an impressive luncheon plate with this torta, encircled by thin red apple slices, juicy orange segments and a cluster of green seedless grapes.

1 1/4 cups sesame cracker crumbs (about 20 crackers)
1/4 cup margarine or butter, melted
1 (8-oz.) package Neufchâtel cheese, at room temperature
4 ounces Roquefort cheese, crumbled
2 eggs
1/2 cup sour cream
1 teaspoon grated onion
1 teaspoon Worcestershire sauce

Combine sesame cracker crumbs and margarine or butter in a small bowl. Reserve 1/3 cup crumb mixture. Press remaining mixture on bottom and halfway up side of a 9-inch pie pan; refrigerate.

Preheat oven to 350F (175C). Beat Neufchâtel and Roquefort cheeses in a medium bowl until well blended. Beat in eggs, sour cream, onion and Worcestershire sauce. Spoon into crumb-lined pan. Sprinkle with reserved crumbs.

Bake 30 to 35 minutes or until just set. Turn off heat and leave in oven with door ajar 30 minutes. Refrigerate overnight or several hours until thoroughly chilled. To serve, cut into wedges.

MAKES 6 TO 8 SERVINGS.

California Quiche

Eye-appealing mini-quiches use familiar flavors dressed up in pastry for a special look. Serve for almost any occasion, from brunch to midnight snacks.

Pastry for a double-crust 9-inch pie
3 eggs
1 cup sour cream, plus extra for garnish
3 tablespoons canned diced green chiles
1/2 cup sliced ripe olives
1/4 cup sliced green onions, plus extra for garnish
6 ounces (1 1/2 cups) Monterey Jack cheese, shredded
1/4 teaspoon salt
1/8 teaspoon pepper

Preheat oven to 375F (190C). On a lightly floured surface, roll pastry into a 16 × 12-inch rectangle. Cut pastry into 12 (4-inch) circles. Ease each pastry circle into a 3-inch quiche pan or 4-inch tart pan, covering bottom and sides. Trim pastry even with top of each pan. Arrange pans on large baking sheet.

Beat eggs in a medium bowl. Stir in 1 cup sour cream, then stir in chiles, olives, 1/4 cup green onions, cheese, salt and pepper. Spoon about 1/4 cup filling into each unbaked pastry shell.

Bake 25 minutes or until filling is set. Remove from oven; let stand in pans about 5 minutes. Loosen pastry from sides; remove quiches from pans. Garnish with sour cream and green onion. Serve warm or at room temperature.

MAKES 12 (3- TO 4-INCH) QUICHES.

Layered Sausage and Mushroom Omelet

A nonstick skillet is ideal for this recipe.

8 ounces pork sausage
Vegetable Filling (see opposite)
8 eggs
3 tablespoons milk
1/4 teaspoon salt
1/8 teaspoon pepper
1 tablespoon vegetable oil
1/2 cup (2 ounces) shredded
   Swiss or Cheddar cheese
Salsa (optional)

Vegetable Filling

1 medium tomato, seeded, peeled
   and chopped
4 mushrooms, sliced
2 green onions, sliced
1 small green chile, chopped

Cook sausage in a medium skillet over medium heat, stirring to break up meat, until meat is browned; drain. Make Vegetable Filling and set aside.

Beat eggs, milk, salt and pepper in a medium bowl until well blended. Heat about 1 teaspoon oil in a 7- or 8-inch skillet over medium heat. Pour 1/3 of egg mixture (about 2/3 cup) into skillet. As eggs set, lift edges with a spatula, allowing uncooked portion to flow underneath. Cook until set; slide out of pan onto a baking sheet with sides. Repeat with remaining egg mixture and oil to make 2 more omelets; set omelets aside on plates.

Preheat broiler. Top omelet on baking sheet with Vegetable Filling. Top with an omelet, then cooked sausage. Top with remaining omelet. Sprinkle with cheese. Broil until cheese melts, about 2 to 3 minutes. Cut into wedges. Serve with salsa, if desired.

Makes 5 or 6 servings.

Vegetable Filling

Combine tomato, mushrooms, onions and chile in a small saucepan. Cook, stirring, over medium heat 4 to 5 minutes; drain.

Small Meals

Alpine Cheese Frittata

A hearty dish that's equally at home for brunch or Sunday night supper.

4 ounces angel hair pasta
8 ounces light kielbasa (Polish sausage), cut into thin slices
1 small onion, chopped
1 clove garlic, crushed
1 carrot, peeled and very thinly sliced
1/4 cup dry, white wine
6 eggs
2 tablespoons milk
1/4 teaspoon salt
1/8 teaspoon pepper
1/2 cup (2 oz.) shredded Swiss cheese

Cook pasta according to package directions; drain, rinse and set aside. Sauté sausage, onion, garlic and carrot in a large skillet over medium heat until vegetables are softened, about 5 minutes. Add wine; cover and simmer 5 to 10 minutes.

Beat eggs and milk in a medium bowl. Add reserved cooked pasta, salt and pepper. Pour over sausage mixture. Sprinkle with cheese. Cover skillet; cook over medium-low heat 10 to 15 minutes or until eggs set. Cut into wedges.

MAKES 5 OR 6 SERVINGS.

Zucchini-Cheese Frittata

It's best to choose a firm tomato such as the Roma (plum) variety. If the tomato is very juicy, drain before adding to other ingredients.

2 tablespoons vegetable or olive oil	1/4 cup all-purpose flour
2 medium zucchini, thinly sliced	1/4 teaspoon salt
1 small onion, thinly sliced	1/8 teaspoon pepper
1 medium tomato, peeled, seeded and chopped	1/3 cup freshly grated Parmesan cheese
4 eggs, beaten slightly	2 teaspoons chopped fresh basil

Preheat oven to 350F (175C). Grease an 8-inch oval or round baking dish; set aside. Heat oil in a 9- or 10-inch skillet over medium heat. Add zucchini and onion and cook, stirring, until vegetables are tender, about 5 minutes. Add tomato.

Combine eggs, flour, salt, pepper and cheese in a medium bowl. Stir in cooked zucchini mixture. Pour into prepared baking dish. Sprinkle with basil. Bake 30 to 35 minutes or until firm. Cut into wedges. Serve warm.

MAKES 5 OR 6 SERVINGS.

Sausage and Eggs with Tortilla Strips

Serve as an appetizing main dish for Sunday brunch. Just add some fresh fruit.

8 ounces bulk pork sausage
6 corn tortillas, halved and cut into 1-inch strips
8 eggs
1/2 cup picante sauce
1/4 cup canned diced green chiles, drained
2 tablespoons chopped fresh cilantro

Cook sausage in a 10-inch skillet over medium heat until browned, stirring to break up. Drain off some of fat. Stir in tortilla strips. Beat eggs in a medium bowl; stir in picante sauce. Add to sausage mixture. Stir in chiles. Cook over medium heat, stirring until eggs are firm. Sprinkle with cilantro.

MAKES 6 TO 8 SERVINGS.

Twice-Baked Potatoes

These favorite baked stuffed potatoes are flavored with turkey sausage and cheese.

4 large baking potatoes
1/3 cup milk
8 ounces bulk turkey sausage
2 teaspoons chopped fresh chives
1/4 teaspoon salt
1/8 teaspoon pepper
1/4 teaspoon chili powder
2 ounces (1/2 cup) Monterey Jack cheese, shredded

Preheat oven to 425F (220C). Bake potatoes about 1 hour or until tender. Cool slightly; halve each potato lengthwise. Scoop out the inside of each half, leaving about 1/4-inch-thick shells. Mash scooped-out potato in a medium bowl; beat in milk.

Cook turkey sausage in a medium skillet over medium heat until no longer pink, stirring to break up sausage, and drain off fat. Add chives, salt, pepper and chili powder. Stir in mashed potatoes. Spoon sausage mixture into potato shells. Sprinkle with cheese. Return stuffed potatoes to oven 10 to 15 minutes or until cheese melts.

MAKES 8 SERVINGS.

Curried Sweet Potato Soup

A fragrant soup with a base of sweet potatoes and a slight curry flavor.

2 large sweet potatoes, peeled and cubed
1 (14- to 16-oz.) can chicken broth
1 onion, chopped
1 teaspoon curry powder
1/4 teaspoon salt
1/8 teaspoon pepper
1 seedless orange, peeled and cubed
2 cups milk or half and half
2 tablespoons margarine or butter
Chopped fresh parsley

Combine sweet potatoes, broth, onion, curry powder, salt and pepper in a 3-quart saucepan over medium heat. Bring to a boil; cover and simmer about 30 minutes or until potatoes are soft.

Pour potatoes and broth into a food processor or blender; add orange and process until smooth. Return to pan; stir in milk or half and half and margarine or butter. Heat until hot and pour into soup bowls. Sprinkle with chopped parsley.

MAKES 4 TO 6 SERVINGS.

All Wrapped Up

Appetizers and small meals that are wrapped in tortillas, wonton wrappers, lettuce leaves and other wrappers are part of a growing trend. With today's busy schedule, having a snack or meal that can be eaten out of hand, and often on the run, has many benefits. No knife and fork are required and these wraps, if made small, are perfect bite-size party foods to serve on picnics, around the pool or in your living room.

Pesto-Style Chicken Fajitas

Although chicken is our first choice for this recipe, we also enjoy substituting beef strips for a change of flavor. The tortillas can be warmed quickly in a microwave oven.

1 cup lightly packed fresh basil leaves
1/4 cup lightly packed fresh parsley leaves
1 clove garlic, chopped
1 tablespoon olive oil
4 ounces (1/2 cup) ricotta cheese, drained
2 tablespoons freshly grated Parmesan cheese
2 boneless, skinless chicken breast halves (about 8 ounces)
1 tablespoon vegetable oil
1 cup sliced broccoli
1/2 cup sliced red bell pepper
1/2 cup sliced canned water chestnuts
1/4 teaspoon salt
1/8 teaspoon black pepper
4 (7-inch) flour tortillas, warmed
2 tablespoons pine nuts

Combine basil, parsley, garlic, olive oil, ricotta cheese, and Parmesan cheese in a blender or food processor. Process until chopped but not pureed; set aside.

Cut chicken into thin strips. In a large skillet or wok, heat vegetable oil over high heat. Add chicken strips and broccoli and stir-fry until chicken is no longer pink in center, about 3 minutes. Stir in bell pepper, water chestnuts, salt, and black pepper and stir-fry until hot. Spoon onto warm tortillas; spoon basil mixture over top. Sprinkle with pine nuts and fold tortillas over filling. Serve warm.

MAKES 4 SERVINGS.

Taste-of-the-Tropics Grilled-Chicken Burritos

To add a smoky flavor to the salsa, grill the chiles first (see Variation) and peel and chop them while the chicken cooks. Warm the tortillas on the grill just before serving.

1/2 cup teriyaki sauce
2 tablespoons vegetable oil
1 tablespoon honey
4 boneless chicken breast halves
2 bananas, unpeeled and halved lengthwise
1 (7- or 8-oz.) can refried beans, heated
4 (7-inch) flour tortillas, warmed
Fruit Salsa (see opposite)

FRUIT SALSA

1 or 2 poblano or green chiles, seeded and sliced
1 (8-oz.) can crushed pineapple, drained
1 medium tomato, peeled, seeded and chopped
1 medium mango, peeled and chopped

Combine teriyaki sauce, oil and honey in a shallow bowl. Add chicken breasts. Cover and refrigerate 2 or 3 hours. Turn chicken breasts; refrigerate another 2 or 3 hours.

Preheat grill. Remove chicken from marinade and arrange on grill rack about 4 inches from heat. Grill chicken about 6 minutes. Turn and grill other side about 4 minutes or until juices run clear when pierced with a fork.

Place bananas, skin side down, on grill with chicken. Brush bananas with chicken marinade and grill until browned on bottom. Turn and grill other side.

Spoon 1/4 of the beans into each tortilla. Add a chicken piece to each tortilla and top with salsa. Fold ends in and roll up. Garnish with bananas.

MAKES 4 SERVINGS.

FRUIT SALSA

Combine chiles, pineapple, tomato, and mango in a medium bowl.

VARIATION

Grill chiles until blistered on all sides. Place in a sealed plastic bag until cool enough to handle. Peel, seed, and chop.

Chicken-Leek Filo Roll-Ups

When cleaning leeks, trim and discard the tough, dark-green tops. Use only white and light-green parts. Be sure to wash leeks well to remove all sand and grit.

2 boneless, skinless chicken breast halves, cut into small pieces (about 8 ounces)
4 ounces prosciutto, chopped
6 tablespoons margarine or butter
1 small leek, cleaned and thinly sliced
2 tablespoons freshly grated Parmesan cheese
2 tablespoons pine nuts, chopped
1/2 teaspoon finely chopped fresh tarragon leaves
1/8 teaspoon pepper
1 egg, beaten slightly
8 sheets filo dough

Preheat oven to 400F (205C). Combine chicken and prosciutto in a food processor. Process until finely chopped, but not pureed. In a large skillet over medium heat, melt 2 tablespoons of the margarine or butter. Add leek; sauté until soft. Stir in chicken mixture; cook, stirring frequently, 10 minutes or until chicken is done. Remove from heat.

Stir in Parmesan cheese, pine nuts, tarragon, pepper and egg. Melt remaining 4 tablespoons margarine or butter. Brush 1 sheet filo with melted margarine or butter; fold in half crosswise and then in half again, resulting in a piece 1/4 of the original size. Turn folded filo so that long side faces you. Place 1/4 cup filling just below center of filo. Roll wrapper a half turn over so filling is covered. Fold in 2 sides to meet in middle. Roll up filo, ending with seam side down. Brush with melted margarine or butter. Repeat with remaining filling and filo.

Place filled rolls on an ungreased baking sheet. Bake 15 to 18 minutes or until golden. Serve hot.

MAKES 8 ROLLS.

Sweet-Hot Turkey Spring Rolls

Try this exciting way to feature cooked turkey at lunch or Sunday night supper.

2 tablespoons soy sauce
2 teaspoons sweet-hot mustard
1 teaspoon honey
1 teaspoon fresh lemon juice
1/2 teaspoon sesame oil
1/4 teaspoon crushed red pepper flakes
2 cups finely chopped cooked turkey or chicken
1/2 cup finely chopped water chestnuts
8 spring roll wrappers
1 tablespoon sesame seeds, toasted (see Note, below)
1/2 cup vegetable oil
Teriyaki or soy sauce, to serve

Combine soy sauce, mustard, honey, lemon juice, sesame oil and pepper flakes in a medium bowl. Add turkey or chicken and water chestnuts. Cover and refrigerate at least 1 hour.

Lightly brush one side of spring roll wrappers with water; sprinkle with sesame seeds. Turn over; brush other side with water. Spoon about 1/4 cup chicken mixture 1 inch from bottom edge of wrapper. Fold sides in 1 inch toward center; roll up from bottom.

Heat vegetable oil in a 10- to 12-inch skillet over medium-high heat. Add filled rolls, cook until browned, turn and brown other side. Serve warm. Dip into teriyaki or soy sauce.

MAKES 8 ROLLS.

NOTE

Preheat oven to 350F (175C). Spread sesame seeds in a 9-inch pie or cake pan. Toast about 5 minutes or until golden. Or, toast in a dry skillet over low heat about 3 or 4 minutes.

Rhineland Mini-Fajitas

A marriage of unusual flavors that spell wunderbar.

2 thick pork loin chops (about 1 to 1 1/2 pounds)
1 teaspoon chili powder
1 clove garlic, crushed
1/2 teaspoon salt
1 tablespoon grated gingerroot
1 tablespoon light brown sugar
1/2 teaspoon grated orange peel
1 teaspoon Dijon mustard
1 tablespoon white-wine vinegar
3 or 4 (9-inch) flour tortillas, quartered
1 tablespoon vegetable oil
1 tablespoon butter
1 medium onion, thinly sliced
1 medium red cooking apple, thinly sliced
1/3 cup sour cream
Ground cinnamon
Orange peel
Parsley sprigs, for garnish

Remove bones from chops; trim off fat. Place chops, 2 inches apart, between 2 sheets of plastic wrap or waxed paper. With a meat mallet, lightly pound pork to almost 1/2-inch thickness. Cut into 1/4-inch-wide strips. Place strips in single layer on a plate.

Combine chili powder, garlic, salt, ginger, brown sugar and orange peel in a small bowl. Stir in mustard and wine vinegar. Lightly brush pork strips with spicy mixture. Cover and refrigerate at least 2 hours.

Just before serving, wrap tortilla quarters in foil; heat in 350F (175C) oven 15 minutes.

Heat oil in a heavy 9-inch skillet. Add pork strips to skillet. Sauté over medium-high heat until no longer pink when cut in thickest part, about 10 minutes; keep warm.

Meanwhile, in another 8- or 9-inch skillet, melt butter over medium-high heat. Add onion and apple; cook, stirring occasionally, 10 minutes or until onion is tender.

To serve, spoon 2 or 3 strips of pork down the center of each tortilla quarter; top with some apple-onion mixture. Roll up and secure with a wooden pick. Top with sour cream, then sprinkle with cinnamon and orange peel. Garnish with parsley sprigs.

MAKES 12 TO 15 APPETIZERS.

Shiitake Pork Spring Rolls

This unusual flavor combination will impress all your friends. Jicama, a large root vegetable with a light brown skin and white interior, is available in Mexican markets and most supermarkets. Peel before using raw or cooked.

4 dried shiitake mushrooms, quartered
1 pound boneless pork cubes
3 green onions, cut into 1-inch pieces
1 tablespoon vegetable oil
1/3 cup finely chopped jicama
2 tablespoons chopped cilantro leaves
1/4 teaspoon salt
10 egg roll wrappers, about 7 inches square
Dipping Sauce (see opposite)
1 1/3 cups vegetable oil, for deep-fat frying

20 leaves leaf lettuce
Mint leaves
Cilantro leaves

Dipping Sauce

1/3 cup rice vinegar
1/4 cup water
1/3 cup sugar
1/4 teaspoon crushed red pepper flakes
1 clove garlic, minced

Cover mushrooms with hot water. Soak about 15 minutes; drain. Combine pork, drained mushrooms and onions in food processor fitted with metal blade. Process until finely chopped.

Heat 1 tablespoon vegetable oil in a medium skillet. Add chopped pork mixture; cook, stirring to break up, until no longer pink. Stir in jicama, chopped cilantro and salt. Place about 1/4 cup filling diagonally on each egg roll wrapper. Fold bottom corner over filling; then fold 2 side corners in toward center. Roll filling toward top corner.

Prepare sauce; set aside. Heat 1 1/3 cups oil in a medium skillet over medium-high heat. Add 3 or 4 egg rolls at a time. Cook and turn until golden on all sides. Drain; halve each roll crosswise. Top each lettuce leaf with several mint leaves and several cilantro leaves and 1 roll half; roll up. Arrange on a platter with dip in the center. Dip rolls in sauce.

Makes 20 appetizers.

Dipping Sauce

Combine all ingredients in a small bowl.

All Wrapped Up

Curried Pork Fold-Overs

Tempting morsels with spicy flavors from Southeast Asia.

3 tablespoons vegetable oil
8 ounces lean ground pork
1 clove garlic, crushed
1 teaspoon curry powder
1 teaspoon grated gingerroot
2 tablespoons flaked coconut

1 tablespoon fruit chutney, fruit pieces finely chopped
1/4 teaspoon salt
1/8 teaspoon pepper
2 tablespoons plain yogurt
22 (3-inch) round wonton wrappers

Heat 1 tablespoon of the oil in a medium skillet over medium heat. Add pork and garlic and cook, stirring to break up pork, until pork is no longer pink. Drain off fat.

Combine drained pork, curry powder, ginger, coconut, chutney, salt and pepper; stir in yogurt.

Spoon about 1 tablespoon filling onto lower half of a wonton wrapper, leaving an uncovered edge. Lightly brush edge of wrapper with water. Fold wrapper over to form a half-moon shape. Press with fork to seal, if desired. Repeat with remaining filling and wonton wrappers.

Heat remaining 2 tablespoons oil in a large skillet over medium heat. Cook half the fold-overs until golden on both sides. Repeat with remaining fold-overs. Serve warm.

MAKES 22 FOLD-OVERS.

Italian Envelopes

A Chinese wonton wrapper around Italian ingredients results in good American eating.

1 egg, beaten slightly
1/2 cup ricotta cheese, drained
2 ounces (1/2 cup) salami, finely chopped
2 ounces (1/2 cup) mozzarella cheese, finely chopped
1/4 teaspoon dried leaf oregano, crushed
1/4 teaspoon salt
1/8 teaspoon pepper
18 to 20 square wonton wrappers
1/4 cup vegetable oil
2 tablespoons freshly grated Parmesan cheese

Combine egg, ricotta cheese, salami, mozzarella cheese, oregano, salt and pepper in a small bowl. Place a wonton wrapper at an angle with 1 corner facing you. Spoon about 1 tablespoon cheese mixture in center of wrapper. Lightly brush edges with water. Fold right and left corners inward, overlapping slightly. Then bring bottom and top corners together, overlapping slightly in middle. Repeat until all ingredients are used.

Heat oil in large skillet over medium-high heat. Fry a single layer of envelopes at a time, turning once, until golden on both sides. Remove from skillet; immediately sprinkle tops with Parmesan cheese. Drain on paper towels. Repeat until all are cooked. Serve warm.

MAKES 18 TO 20 APPETIZERS.

Korean Omelet Wraps

These are very thin omelets that are picked up and eaten. The vegetable filling was inspired by a Korean recipe. We like tortillas with it, so we decided to use them as wrappers.

1 tablespoon vegetable oil	2 tablespoons thinly sliced green onion
2 teaspoons sesame oil	1/4 teaspoon salt
1 small zucchini, cut into 2-inch matchsticks	1/2 cup bean sprouts
1/2 large red bell pepper, cut into 2-inch matchsticks	6 eggs, beaten slightly
	2 tablespoons soy sauce
1 jalapeño chile, seeded and finely chopped	2 tablespoons margarine or butter
	4 (8-inch) flour tortillas, warmed

Heat vegetable oil and sesame oil in an 8- or 9-inch skillet over medium heat. Add zucchini, red bell pepper, jalapeño chile and green onion. Cook, stirring occasionally, about 5 minutes, until vegetables are soft but not completely soft. Stir in salt and bean sprouts. Remove from heat; cool slightly.

Beat eggs in a medium bowl; stir in soy sauce and cooked vegetables. Melt 1/2 tablespoon margarine or butter in skillet over medium-low heat. Spoon 1/4 of the vegetable-egg mixture into skillet. Evenly spread out vegetables with back of a spoon. Cook 5 minutes, until golden on both sides. Repeat with remaining margarine or butter and vegetable-egg mixture.

Place a cooked vegetable omelet on each warm tortilla. Roll up; serve immediately.

MAKES 4 SERVINGS.

Filo-Asparagus Fingers

Baking these seam side up helps keep the cheese from oozing out during cooking.

4 sheets filo dough
1/3 cup margarine or butter, melted
2 tablespoons sweet-hot mustard
1/4 teaspoon paprika

16 asparagus spears, cooked
2 ounces Brie cheese, cut into
  16 small strips

Preheat oven to 400F (205C). Cut long side of each sheet of filo dough into 4 lengthwise pieces to get 16 strips about 14 × 4 1/2 inches.

Combine margarine or butter, mustard and paprika in a small bowl; brush on top side of filo strips. Place 1 cooked asparagus spear and a strip of Brie crosswise near end of each filo strip. Roll up jelly-roll style, starting at end with asparagus; place seam side up in a shallow baking pan.

Bake 6 to 8 minutes or until filo is golden brown. Serve immediately.

MAKES 16 SERVINGS.

Bean and Goat-Cheese Quesadillas

Crispy tortillas are filled with an exciting mixture of vegetables accented with spices.

2 slices bacon, diced
1 (15-oz.) can kidney beans
3/4 teaspoon ground cumin
1 jalapeño chile, seeded and finely chopped
1 zucchini, shredded
1 small onion, chopped
1 clove garlic, finely chopped
10 (5-inch) flour tortillas
1 cup (about 4 ounces) crumbled goat cheese
1/2 cup chopped red onion
1 carrot, peeled and grated
3 to 4 tablespoons vegetable oil

Cook bacon in a medium skillet over medium heat until slightly crisp. Drain beans, reserving 1/4 cup liquid. Partially mash beans, then add to cooked bacon. Stir in cumin, jalapeño chile, zucchini, onion and garlic; simmer 2 to 3 minutes. If mixture is too dry, add some of the reserved bean liquid.

Spread about 2 tablespoons bean mixture on half of each tortilla. Top each with 1 generous tablespoon goat cheese, about 2 teaspoons red onion and about 1 tablespoon carrot. Fold each in a half-moon shape.

Heat 2 tablespoons oil in a large skillet or griddle over medium heat. Cook 3 or 4 filled tortillas at a time until golden, turning as needed. Repeat, adding additional oil as necessary, until all filled tortillas are cooked. Serve warm.

MAKES 10 SERVINGS.

Stuffed Grape Leaves

Buy grape leaves in the jar in gourmet food stores or ethnic sections of supermarkets.

1 (8-oz.) jar grape leaves in brine
1/4 cup olive oil or vegetable oil
1 onion, chopped
1/2 cup rice
2 tablespoons pine nuts
1 cup chicken broth or bouillon
1/4 cup chopped fresh parsley
1/2 teaspoon salt
1/8 teaspoon pepper
1 tablespoon fresh lemon juice
1/8 teaspoon ground allspice
2 tablespoons dried currants
Lemon slices, for garnish

Gently separate grape leaves; rinse in warm water. Select 35 to 40 full leaves without tears; reserve remaining leaves. Cut stems from selected leaves; set leaves aside.

Heat oil in a medium skillet over medium heat. Add onion and sauté until softened, about 5 minutes. Add rice and pine nuts; sauté until lightly browned, about 5 minutes. Stir in broth or bouillon, parsley, salt, pepper, lemon juice and allspice. Cover and simmer over low heat 15 minutes or until rice is tender. Stir in currants; set rice mixture aside.

Place a metal rack in bottom of a large kettle or Dutch oven. Make a bed of imperfect reserved leaves on rack. Place trimmed leaves on a flat surface, vein side up and stem end toward you. Spoon 1 1/2 to 2 tablespoons rice mixture on stem end of each leaf. Fold right and left sides over rice mixture and roll up as tightly as possible jelly-roll style. Stack stuffed leaves very close together over bed of leaves. Place a heavy plate or dish on top of stuffed grape leaves to hold rolls in place.

Cover stuffed leaves with hot water. Cover and simmer over low heat 45 to 50 minutes. Remove cooked rolls from water, discarding water; set stuffed leaves aside to cool. Arrange stuffed leaves on a platter. Garnish with lemon slices.

MAKES 35 TO 40 APPETIZERS.

Shrimp and Black Bean Wraps

Put together this hearty combination for a filling meal-in-a-tortilla.

1 pound large raw shrimp, peeled
2 medium onions, cut crosswise into 1/2-inch-thick slices
1 cup bottled salsa
1 (15-oz.) can black beans, drained and rinsed
1 medium red bell pepper, cut into 1 1/2 × 1/4-inch strips
4 (10-inch) flour tortillas, warmed
1/4 cup sour cream

Lightly grease grill or skillet and heat over medium-high heat. Brush shrimp and onion slices with salsa. Grill 1 to 2 minutes or until cooked on 1 side. Brush with salsa; turn and grill on other side another 1 to 2 minutes or until shrimp are pink and firm.

Meanwhile, heat black beans and bell pepper in a medium saucepan over low heat. Spoon cooked shrimp, onions and bean mixture into each warm flour tortilla. Top with sour cream. Fold in sides of tortilla; roll up.

MAKES 4 SERVINGS.

Falafel Taco Wraps

Cucumber sauce is at its best when eaten soon after preparation.

1 (15 1/2-oz.) can garbanzo beans, drained and rinsed
1 egg
1 tablespoon fresh lemon juice
3 tablespoons fine dry bread crumbs
2 tablespoons chopped fresh parsley
1/4 teaspoon black pepper
1/4 teaspoon cayenne pepper
1/2 teaspoon salt
1/4 cup vegetable oil
1/2 cup plain yogurt
1 small cucumber, peeled, seeded and shredded
1 tablespoon chopped fresh cilantro
4 (6-inch) corn or flour tortillas, warmed

Combine beans, egg and lemon juice in a food processor or blender. Process until finely ground. Add bread crumbs, parsley, black pepper, cayenne pepper and salt and process to combine.

Heat oil in an 8-inch skillet over medium-high heat. With wet hands, form bean mixture into 4 logs about 6 × 1 inch, using about 1/3 cup for each. Cook 2 logs at a time, turning to brown all sides. Drain on paper towels.

Combine yogurt, cucumber and cilantro in a small bowl. Place 1 falafel in center of each tortilla. Top each with about 1/4 cup cucumber sauce. Fold over; serve immediately.

MAKES 6 SERVINGS.

Ham 'n' Egg Wrap 'n' Go

Try an exciting new treat for a special breakfast or brunch.

3 hard-cooked eggs, peeled and chopped
1/2 cup finely chopped cooked ham
1 tablespoon finely chopped green onion
1/4 cup chopped snow peas

1 teaspoon Dijon mustard
1 tablespoon finely chopped fruit chutney
1/4 teaspoon curry powder
6 spring-roll wrappers
1/4 cup vegetable oil

Combine chopped eggs, ham, green onion, snow peas, mustard, chutney and curry in a medium bowl. Spoon about 1/3 cup into center of each spring-roll wrapper. Fold ends over, then roll up. Moisten ends to seal. Heat oil in an 8-inch skillet over medium heat. Add rolls and brown rolls on both sides.

MAKES 6 ROLLS.

Risotto Pinwheel Wraps

To simplify preparation of this hearty snack or sandwich with favorite Italian ingredients, start with a rice mix.

1 (5.7-ounce) carton mushroom risotto mix
1 cup (8 ounces) ricotta cheese, drained
1 large (22 × 13-inch) sheet soft Armenian cracker bread
2 tablespoons chopped fresh basil
12 large fresh spinach leaves
8 ounces sliced mortadella
4 ounces thinly sliced salami
6 ounces sliced provolone cheese

Prepare risotto according to package directions; set aside to cool.

Spread ricotta cheese evenly on bread. Sprinkle with basil, then cover with spinach leaves. Arrange mortadella, salami and provolone over spinach. Carefully spread top with risotto. Starting at long side, roll up tightly. For a main-dish serving, cut crosswise into 4 to 6 pieces, or cut into 12 to 14 slices for appetizers. Serve now or cover and refrigerate 1 to 2 hours.

MAKES 4 TO 6 MAIN-DISH SERVINGS OR 12 TO 14 APPETIZERS.

Thai Curried Turkey Wraps

If turkey is not available, substitute 1 pound of boneless, skinless chicken pieces.

3 tablespoons vegetable oil
1 teaspoon curry powder
1 tablespoon fresh lemon juice
1 clove garlic, crushed
1 tablespoon honey
1 pound boneless uncooked turkey breast, cut into 1 1/2 × 1/2-inch strips
1/2 cup peanut butter
1 tablespoon soy sauce
1/2 cup chicken broth
1/4 teaspoon crushed red pepper flakes
2 medium carrots, peeled and very thinly sliced
1 onion, cut into 12 wedges
1 cup sugar snap peas, halved crosswise
2 cups warm cooked jasmine rice
5 or 6 (10-inch) whole-wheat or white flour tortillas

Combine 2 tablespoons of the oil, curry powder, lemon juice, garlic and honey in a medium bowl. Stir in turkey; cover and refrigerate 2 to 3 hours or overnight.

Whisk together peanut butter, soy sauce, broth and pepper flakes; set aside.

Heat remaining tablespoon oil in a medium skillet over medium-high heat. Add carrots, onion and turkey mixture. Cook, stirring, until turkey is done, 5 to 10 minutes. Stir in peas; cook 1 minute. Place about 1/3 cup cooked warm rice on center of each tortilla.

Top each tortilla with about 1 cup turkey-vegetable mixture. Drizzle with 2 or 3 tablespoons peanut butter sauce. Fold ends in and roll up.

MAKES 5 OR 6 SERVINGS.

Salads

Salads fit into all kinds of versatile menus. A hearty main-dish salad such as Barbados Black Bean 'n' Rice Turkey Salad or Bali Hai–Style Couscous offers a welcome change of pace from the typical dinner menu. One of these salads can be used as the base of an exciting and satisfying small meal or as the complete meal. Then you can add other dishes that blend with it.

Or try a pasta salad with a hint of Italian influence or a flavorful exotic combination reminiscent of Asian flavors as the main dish. When you borrow from a variety of cuisines, the results are usually exciting and appealing to most people.

Choose the freshest ingredients for your salads—the crispest vegetables and ripe juicy tomatoes. Extra-virgin olive oil will add rich flavor to dressings.

Honey-Curried Chicken and Orzo Salad

Save time by cooking the chicken and onion ahead of time; refrigerate until just before adding to other ingredients.

1/4 cup shredded sweetened coconut
2 tablespoons vegetable oil
1 pound boneless, skinless chicken or turkey, cubed
2 green onions, sliced
1 clove garlic, crushed
1/2 cup orzo
1 1/2 teaspoons curry powder
1/2 teaspoon ground ginger
1/4 teaspoon salt
1 small jicama, peeled and julienned
1 small red apple, cored and chopped

HONEY DRESSING

1/4 cup red-wine vinegar
1 tablespoon honey
1 tablespoon Dijon mustard
1/4 teaspoon salt
1/8 teaspoon pepper
1/4 cup vegetable oil

Preheat oven to 350F (175C). Spread coconut in a 9-inch pie or cake pan. Toast about 6 to 8 minutes or until golden; set aside to cool.

Heat oil in a large skillet over medium heat. Add chicken or turkey, onions and garlic. Cook, stirring, until poultry is no longer pink, about 10 minutes; cool.

Cook orzo according to package directions; drain. Stir in curry powder, ginger, salt and cooked chicken mixture; refrigerate.

At serving time, combine cooked chicken and orzo mixture with jicama and apple. Prepare dressing and pour over salad. Toss until well mixed. Top with toasted coconut.

MAKES 4 TO 6 SERVINGS.

HONEY DRESSING

Whisk together all ingredients in a small bowl.

Taste-of-Thai Bowl

Chinese cabbage teams with lettuce to provide a base for this flavorful combination of tropical fruits with chicken.

2 cups shredded Chinese cabbage
2 cups shredded lettuce
1 mango, peeled, pitted and cubed
2 cups fresh pineapple chunks (1/2 small pineapple)
4 boneless, skinless chicken breast halves, grilled and cut into small strips
3 tablespoons hoisin sauce
2 tablespoons white-wine vinegar
1 teaspoon grated gingerroot
1 tablespoon light brown sugar
1 teaspoon soy sauce
1/2 cup plain low-fat yogurt
1 tablespoon sesame seeds, toasted (see Note, page 109)

Combine Chinese cabbage and lettuce in a large salad bowl. Top with mango, pineapple and grilled chicken.

Combine hoisin sauce, vinegar, ginger, brown sugar and soy sauce in a small dish. Stir into yogurt. Pour over chicken and other ingredients in salad bowl. Toss until combined. Sprinkle with sesame seeds.

MAKES 4 TO 6 SERVINGS.

Hearty Pasta Salad Bowl

Just serve your favorite rolls or bread with this salad for a satisfying meal.

8 ounces angel hair pasta
2 tablespoons vegetable oil
1 clove garlic, halved
1 pound boneless, skinned turkey breast, cut into thin strips
2 small zucchini, cut into strips about 2 inches long
2 medium tomatoes, chopped
2 cups (about 10 oz.) chopped cooked ham
1/4 teaspoon salt
1/8 teaspoon pepper
4 ounces (1 cup) Monterey Jack cheese, diced
1/4 cup chopped fresh basil

Cook pasta according to package directions; drain and set aside.

Heat oil and garlic in large skillet over medium heat until fragrant. Remove and discard garlic. Add turkey; sauté 3 or 4 minutes or until no longer pink. Stir in zucchini, tomatoes and ham. Cook until zucchini is tender, about 3 minutes; set aside.

Combine pasta, salt, pepper, cheese and fresh basil in a large bowl. Add turkey, vegetables and liquid from skillet. Toss until well blended.

MAKES 4 TO 6 SERVINGS.

Sun-Dried Tomato Pasta

The combination of sun-dried and fresh tomatoes produces exceptionally good flavor.

3/4 cup sun-dried tomatoes (oil packed), drained and chopped
2 small fresh plum tomatoes, chopped
1/4 cup loosely packed, chopped fresh basil
1 clove garlic, crushed
1 tablespoon chopped fresh oregano
2 tablespoons chopped fresh parsley
2 tablespoons olive oil
8 ounces ziti or corkscrew pasta
1/3 cup prepared refrigerated creamy garlic salad dressing
2 to 4 tablespoons freshly grated Parmesan cheese

Combine dried and fresh tomatoes, basil, garlic, oregano, parsley and oil in a medium bowl. Cover and refrigerate while cooking pasta.

Cook pasta according to package directions; drain and cool. Add refrigerated dressing to pasta; toss until well blended. Top with cheese.

MAKES 4 TO 6 SERVINGS.

Pasta à la Pesto

You'll find all your favorite Italian seasonings, including Gorgonzola cheese, in this wonderful pasta dish.

8 ounces linguine or other thin pasta
1 cup lightly packed basil leaves
1/2 cup olive or vegetable oil
1 clove garlic, peeled
2 tablespoons chopped fresh Italian parsley
1/4 cup pine nuts, toasted (see page 205)
1/4 teaspoon salt
1/8 teaspoon pepper
1/4 cup light cream
1/4 cup freshly grated Parmesan cheese
1/4 cup crumbled Gorgonzola cheese

Cook pasta according to package directions; drain and set aside.

Combine basil, oil, garlic, parsley, pine nuts, salt and pepper in a blender or food processor. Process until finely chopped. Stir in cream and Parmesan cheese. Pour over cooked pasta; toss until well blended. Top with Gorgonzola cheese.

MAKES 4 TO 6 SERVINGS.

Eat-with-Your-Hands Italian Salad

The diameter of mortadella or salami determines the number of servings. If possible, purchase large thin slices of meat that can be neatly wrapped around the filling.

1/2 cup orzo pasta	1 tablespoon finely chopped fresh parsley
1 carrot, shredded	1 clove garlic, crushed
1 medium zucchini, chopped	1/2 teaspoon dry mustard
1 medium tomato, chopped	1/2 teaspoon salt
2 ounces (1/2 cup) mozzarella cheese, diced	1/8 teaspoon pepper
2 tablespoons olive oil or vegetable oil	12 to 16 large thin slices of mortadella or salami
2 tablespoons tarragon vinegar	

Cook pasta according to package directions; drain.

Combine cooked pasta, carrot, zucchini, tomato and cheese in a medium bowl.

Whisk together oil, vinegar, parsley, garlic, mustard, salt and pepper in a small bowl. Pour oil mixture over pasta and vegetables; toss to coat well. Cover and refrigerate at least 2 hours.

Place 3 to 4 tablespoons vegetable mixture in center of each large slice of meat. Roll up, securing with a wooden pick if necessary.

MAKES 12 TO 16 SALAD ROLL-UPS.

Bali Hai–Style Couscous

Sometimes packages of couscous may be labeled as Moroccan pasta.

2 1/4 cups chicken bouillon or broth
1 (10-oz.) package couscous
1/4 cup soy sauce
1/4 cup fresh lemon juice
1/4 cup vegetable oil
2 tablespoons chopped fresh chives
1 tablespoon grated gingerroot
1/2 fresh pineapple (2 cups), peeled and diced
1 papaya, peeled, seeded and sliced
1/4 cup chopped macadamia nuts

Bring bouillon or broth to a boil in a medium saucepan. Stir in couscous. Cover and remove from heat; let stand 5 minutes. Stir in soy sauce, lemon juice, oil, chives and ginger. Set aside until cool.

Stir in pineapple. Spoon into serving platter or individual plates. Arrange papaya around couscous mixture. Sprinkle with macadamia nuts.

MAKES ABOUT 6 SERVINGS.

Fruited Rice Salad

An interesting accompaniment to grilled chicken or roast pork.

1 cup long-grain white rice
1/4 cup currants
1 red apple, chopped
1/2 cup orange-flavored low-fat yogurt
2 tablespoons vegetable oil
1 tablespoon white-wine vinegar
1 teaspoon curry powder
1/2 teaspoon turmeric
1 tablespoon chopped fresh cilantro leaves
1/2 teaspoon salt
1/8 teaspoon pepper
2 tablespoons pine nuts, toasted (see page 205)

Cook rice according to package directions; stir in currants and apple. Set aside until cool.

Whisk together yogurt, oil, vinegar, curry powder, turmeric, cilantro, salt and pepper. Add to cooled rice mixture and toss until combined. Sprinkle with toasted pine nuts.

MAKES 4 TO 5 SERVINGS.

Peppered Rice Salad with Goat Cheese

This colorful salad is equally delicious as a main dish for a luncheon, or as an accompaniment to grilled meats at your next barbecue.

1 cup long-grain white rice
2 cups chicken broth or bouillon
1 red or yellow bell pepper
1 green bell pepper
1/3 cup olive oil or vegetable oil
2 tablespoons vinegar

1 tablespoon chopped fresh basil
1 teaspoon chopped fresh marjoram
1/4 teaspoon salt
1/8 teaspoon pepper
1/4 cup crumbled goat cheese

Cook rice with broth or bouillon according to package directions. Refrigerate at least 2 hours or until cold.

Preheat oven to 425F (220C). Halve bell peppers; remove inner membranes and seeds. Place cut side down on a shallow baking pan. Roast 15 to 20 minutes or until skins are wrinkled and dark. Remove and discard skins; cut peppers into thin slivers. Stir into chilled rice.

Whisk together oil, vinegar, herbs, salt and pepper in a small bowl. Pour over rice mixture. Toss until well mixed. Sprinkle with goat cheese.

MAKES 4 TO 5 SERVINGS.

Barbados Black Bean 'n' Rice Turkey Salad

Serve it at a refreshing summertime luncheon or take to your pot-luck dinner.

- 2 cups cooked rice (about 2/3 cup uncooked)
- 1 (15-oz.) can black beans, drained and rinsed
- 2 cups cubed cooked turkey or chicken
- 1 small red onion, sliced
- 1 yellow or green bell pepper, diced
- 1 cup cherry tomatoes, quartered
- 1/4 cup vegetable oil
- 2 tablespoons fresh lemon or lime juice
- 1 tablespoon Dijon mustard
- 1 tablespoon chopped fresh cilantro
- 1 teaspoon honey
- 1/4 teaspoon ground cumin
- 1/4 teaspoon salt
- 1/8 teaspoon pepper

Combine rice, beans, turkey, onion, bell pepper and cherry tomatoes in a large bowl.

Whisk together oil, lemon juice, mustard, cilantro, honey, cumin, salt and pepper in a small bowl. Pour over rice mixture; toss until well mixed.

MAKES ABOUT 6 MAIN-DISH OR 10 SIDE SALADS OR FIRST COURSES.

Kaleidoscope Bean Toss

As its name indicates, this is a colorful dramatic presentation of fresh and canned vegetables, accented with smoked sausage.

1 (16-oz.) can black beans, drained and rinsed
2 tomatoes, peeled and coarsely chopped
1 green or orange bell pepper, coarsely chopped
1 (12-oz.) can whole-kernel corn, drained
1 small onion, diced
4 ounces smoked sausage, thinly sliced
1/2 cup vegetable oil
1/4 cup red-wine vinegar
1 tablespoon Dijon mustard
1 tablespoon honey
1/4 teaspoon salt
1/8 teaspoon pepper
Chopped fresh cilantro

Combine beans, tomatoes, bell pepper, corn, onion and smoked sausage in a large bowl.

Whisk oil, vinegar, mustard, honey, salt and pepper in a small bowl. Pour over bean mixture; toss until combined. Sprinkle with cilantro.

Makes 6 to 8 servings.

Wild West Salad

Very hearty, yet quick and easy, this salad is especially appealing to men. Add the avocado just before serving.

- 1 (15-oz.) can yellow hominy, drained and rinsed
- 1 (15-oz.) can pinto beans, drained and rinsed
- 1 small onion, chopped
- 1/4 cup sweet pickle relish
- 1/2 cup chopped celery
- 4 slices cooked bacon, drained and crumbled
- 3 ounces (3/4 cup) sharp Cheddar cheese, cut into small cubes
- 1/2 cup sour cream
- 2 tablespoons milk
- 1 teaspoon prepared mustard
- 1/2 teaspoon prepared horseradish
- 1/4 teaspoon crushed red pepper flakes
- 1 avocado, peeled, pitted and sliced

Combine hominy, beans, onion, relish, celery, bacon and cheese in a large bowl.

Whisk together sour cream, milk, mustard, horseradish and pepper flakes in a small bowl. Add to hominy mixture. Toss until combined. Top with avocado slices.

MAKES 6 TO 8 SERVINGS.

NOTE

If salad is not served immediately, dip avocado slices in a lemon juice–water mixture to prevent discoloration.

Deli–Potato Salad Wrap-Ups

Stop by your favorite delicatessen and choose several special kinds of cold cuts.

3 medium potatoes, cooked, peeled and cut into julienne strips
4 ounces (1 cup) Cheddar cheese, diced
1/2 cup diced celery
1/2 cup mayonnaise
1 tablespoon prepared mustard
1 teaspoon prepared horseradish
1 tablespoon white-wine vinegar
1 teaspoon sugar
1 teaspoon salt
1/4 teaspoon pepper
15 to 20 large thin slices salami or other sliced cold cuts

Combine potato strips, cheese and celery in a large bowl.

Stir together mayonnaise, mustard, horseradish, vinegar, sugar, salt and pepper in a small bowl. Spoon mayonnaise mixture over potato mixture and toss gently to combine. Cover and refrigerate at least 2 hours.

Spoon 2 to 3 tablespoons potato salad along center of each salami slice; roll up. Serve immediately.

MAKES 15 TO 20 SERVINGS.

Nordic Potato Salad

Cook salmon and potatoes several hours before serving, to allow time for chilling.

8 ounces salmon fillets
10 to 12 small (1 1/2 to 2 inches in diameter) new potatoes
1 small cucumber
1 small red onion, thinly sliced
1 cup plain low-fat yogurt
1 tablespoon Dijon mustard
1 teaspoon dried dill weed
2 tablespoons chopped watercress leaves
1/2 teaspoon salt
1/8 teaspoon pepper

Cook salmon in simmering water until it just begins to flake, about 8 minutes, depending on thickness. Drain and cool in refrigerator. Cook whole unpeeled potatoes in boiling water until tender, about 10 minutes. Drain and cool in refrigerator.

Break salmon into 1/2-inch pieces; set aside. Quarter potatoes, but do not peel. Peel cucumber; halve lengthwise. With a teaspoon, scoop out and discard seeds. Slice cucumber crosswise. Combine potatoes, cucumber and onion in a large bowl.

Stir together yogurt, mustard, dill, watercress, salt and pepper in a small bowl. Pour over potato mixture. Toss until combined. Top with salmon.

MAKES 5 OR 6 SERVINGS.

Fennel and Oranges with Lemon Vinaigrette

A refreshing, multicolored side salad to liven up a VIP dinner.

1 fennel bulb, thinly sliced crosswise
3 oranges, peeled and sliced crosswise
1/3 cup olive or vegetable oil
2 tablespoons white-wine vinegar
1 tablespoon fresh lemon juice
1 teaspoon honey
1 tablespoon chopped fresh cilantro
1/4 teaspoon salt
1/8 teaspoon pepper
1 head butter or Bibb lettuce, separated into leaves
1 small red onion, thinly sliced

Combine sliced fennel and oranges in a large bowl.

Whisk together oil, vinegar, lemon juice, honey, cilantro, salt and pepper in a small bowl. Pour over fennel and oranges. Cover; refrigerate several hours or overnight.

Drain fennel mixture, discarding dressing. Line a large platter or individual salad plates with lettuce, top with drained fennel and oranges; then slices of red onion.

MAKES 4 TO 6 SERVINGS.

Adriatic Antipasto

This is an easy-to-assemble combination for a special luncheon or buffet antipasto salad.

2 cups (about 7 ounces) sliced fresh mushrooms
3 ounces thinly sliced prosciutto, cut into bite-size pieces
2 (6-oz.) jars marinated artichoke heart halves or quarters, drained
4 ounces provolone cheese, julienned
1 red bell pepper, thinly sliced
1/4 cup olive oil
2 tablespoons balsamic vinegar
1 tablespoon finely chopped fresh tarragon
1 teaspoon minced fresh chives
1/4 teaspoon salt
1/8 teaspoon pepper
Lettuce or curly endive leaves

Combine all ingredients except lettuce in a large bowl; toss until combined. Cover and refrigerate several hours.

Line individual salad bowls or plates with lettuce or curly endive. Drain salad and spoon over greens.

MAKES 5 OR 6 SERVINGS.

Artichoke Plate

The actual number of servings depends on whether the jars of artichoke bottoms contain 5 or 6 bottoms.

3 hard-cooked eggs
1/2 cup mayonnaise
1/4 cup plain low-fat yogurt
1 teaspoon Dijon mustard
2 teaspoons dried dill weed
2 teaspoons chopped fresh chives
1/4 teaspoon salt
1/8 teaspoon pepper

10 to 12 Boston or Bibb lettuce leaves
1 (14-oz.) can artichoke bottoms, drained and rinsed
6 to 8 ounces cooked shredded crabmeat
Small pear-shaped tomatoes, for garnish

Combine 1 hard-cooked egg yolk, mayonnaise, yogurt, mustard, dill weed, chives, salt and pepper in a food processor or blender; process until smooth.

Line 5 or 6 large individual salad plates with lettuce leaves. Place 1 artichoke bottom on each plate; top each with crabmeat. Spoon mayonnaise mixture over crabmeat. Slice remaining cooked egg white and hard-cooked eggs; arrange around artichoke bottom. Garnish with small tomatoes.

MAKES 5 OR 6 SERVINGS.

Tomato-Zucchini Mousse

An appealing mold to serve with an assortment of cold sliced meats and cheeses, it can be made ahead and unmolded just before serving.

1 cup tomato juice
1 (1/4-oz.) envelope unflavored gelatin
2 tablespoons margarine or butter
1 small onion, chopped
1 clove garlic, crushed
2 fresh medium tomatoes, peeled, seeded and chopped
1 carrot, peeled and shredded
1 zucchini, shredded
2 teaspoons finely chopped fresh basil
1 teaspoon chopped chives
1 tablespoon chopped parsley
1/2 teaspoon salt
1/8 teaspoon pepper
Lettuce

Pour tomato juice into a small nonreactive saucepan. Sprinkle gelatin over tomato juice; let stand about 1 minute. Heat and stir over low heat until dissolved. In a medium skillet, melt margarine or butter over medium heat. Add onion and garlic; cook and stir several minutes. Remove from heat; stir in chopped tomatoes, carrot, zucchini, basil, chives, parsley, salt, pepper and tomato juice mixture. Pour into 4-cup mold. Refrigerate several hours or until firm. Unmold on lettuce.

MAKES 5 OR 6 SERVINGS.

Breads and Sandwiches

Miniature sandwiches with exotic fillings of poultry, meats or cheese have always been symbolic of special gatherings such as wedding receptions, graduations or anniversaries. They can be served open-faced or made into a checkerboard, ribbon or roll-up shapes. Most of them start with thinly sliced sandwich bread that you can find in your bakery or supermarket.

For an interesting presentation, cut some of the open-face sandwiches into interesting shapes such as triangles, hearts or other designs.

To make cutting bread easier, place unsliced bread in the freezer for about 30 minutes. This is long enough for bread to become firmer and easier to cut, but not long enough for it to freeze solid.

Homemade loaves such as Apple Cheese Brunch Loaf or Sweet Potato Pecan Bread are sure to spark any reception or party menu.

Topsy-Turvy Maple-Walnut Pumpkin Muffins

All the wonderful aromatic spices we associate with pumpkin pie, plus a yummy sticky topping.

12 walnut halves
6 tablespoons light brown sugar
2 tablespoons margarine or butter, melted
1 tablespoon maple syrup
1 cup bran cereal
1 cup buttermilk
1 egg, beaten slightly
1 cup all-purpose flour

2 teaspoons baking powder
1/2 teaspoon baking soda
1/4 teaspoon salt
1/2 teaspoon ground cinnamon
1/8 teaspoon ground ginger
1/4 teaspoon ground nutmeg
2 tablespoons vegetable oil
1/2 cup canned pumpkin

Preheat oven to 400F (205C). Place 1 walnut half in bottom of 12 (2 1/2-inch) muffin cups. Combine 2 tablespoons of the brown sugar, melted margarine or butter and maple syrup in a small bowl. Spoon mixture over each walnut half.

Combine bran cereal and buttermilk in a medium bowl. Stir in egg, flour, remaining 4 tablespoons brown sugar, baking powder, baking soda, salt, cinnamon, ginger, nutmeg, oil and pumpkin just until flour is moistened. Spoon batter over sugar mixture in muffin cups.

Bake about 20 minutes or until tops spring back when lightly touched with your fingertip. Loosen muffins from sides of cups; invert immediately on a cooling rack and let stand about 5 minutes before removing pan. Serve warm or cool.

MAKES 12 MUFFINS.

Herb-Parmesan Muffins

Fresh herbs will produce the best flavor, but about one-third the amount of dried herbs can be substituted.

2 eggs
1 cup milk
1/4 cup vegetable oil
1/4 cup finely chopped sun-dried tomatoes (oil packed), drained
2 cups all-purpose flour
2 teaspoons baking powder
3/4 teaspoon salt
1/2 teaspoon baking soda
1 tablespoon finely chopped fresh basil
1 tablespoon finely chopped fresh oregano
1 tablespoon finely chopped fresh parsley
4 tablespoons freshly grated Parmesan cheese

Preheat oven to 400F (205C). Grease 12 (2 1/2-inch) muffin cups. Beat eggs in a small bowl. Stir in milk, oil and tomatoes.

Combine flour, baking powder, salt, baking soda, basil, oregano, parsley and 2 tablespoons of the Parmesan cheese. Stir in egg mixture just until dry ingredients are moistened. Spoon mixture into greased muffin cups. Sprinkle with the remaining 2 tablespoons Parmesan cheese.

Bake 20 to 22 minutes or until golden brown. Loosen muffins from sides of cups; remove to a cooling rack. Serve warm.

MAKES 12 MUFFINS.

VARIATION

MINI HERB-PARMESAN MUFFINS

Use 1 3/4-inch miniature muffin cups and reduce baking time to 12 to 15 minutes.

MAKES ABOUT 36 MINIATURE MUFFINS.

Breads and Sandwiches

Jalapeño Corn Muffins

Jalapeño chile lends a pleasant "hot" touch. For a milder-flavored muffin, use a mild green chile instead.

1 egg
1/2 cup milk
2 tablespoons vegetable oil
4 ounces (1 cup) Monterey Jack cheese, finely chopped
1 (8-oz.) can cream-style corn
2 tablespoons chopped green onion
1 jalapeño chile, seeded and finely chopped
1/4 teaspoon baking soda
1/4 teaspoon salt
1 cup yellow cornmeal

Preheat oven to 400F (205C). Grease 12 (2 1/2-inch) muffin cups. Beat egg in a medium bowl. Stir in milk, oil, cheese, corn, green onion and jalapeño chile. Stir in baking soda, salt and cornmeal just until moistened. Spoon into greased muffin cups.

Bake 20 to 22 minutes or until golden brown. Loosen muffins from sides of cups; invert on a cooling rack. Serve warm.

MAKES 12 MUFFINS.

Apricot-Cheesecake Muffins

Although paper muffin-cup liners are handy for some muffins, this recipe works better if cups are greased rather than lined.

1/2 cup finely chopped dried apricots
2 tablespoons orange liqueur
2 tablespoons margarine or butter, at room temperature
1 (3-oz.) package cream cheese, at room temperature
1/4 cup sugar
1 egg
1 cup milk
2 cups all-purpose flour
2 teaspoons baking powder
1/4 teaspoon baking soda
1/4 teaspoon salt
1/2 teaspoon grated lemon peel

Preheat oven to 400F (205C). Grease 12 (2 1/2-inch) muffin cups. Combine apricots and liqueur in a small bowl; set aside.

Beat margarine or butter, cream cheese and sugar in a large bowl until creamy. Beat in egg and milk. Stir in flour, baking powder, baking soda, salt, and lemon peel. Stir in liqueur-soaked apricots and any remaining liqueur in bowl. Spoon batter into greased muffin cups.

Bake 20 to 22 minutes or until edges begin to brown. Loosen muffins from sides of cups; invert on a cooling rack.

MAKES 12 MUFFINS.

Sweet Potato Pecan Bread

Inside and outside, the bread is a beautiful golden-brown color, thanks to sweet potatoes and all the flavorful spices. Serve plain or with butter or cream cheese.

1/2 cup margarine or butter, at room temperature
1 cup sugar
2 eggs
2 medium sweet potatoes, baked, peeled and mashed (about 1 cup)
1 1/2 cups all-purpose flour
1 teaspoon baking soda
1/2 teaspoon baking powder
1/2 teaspoon ground cinnamon
1/4 teaspoon ground cloves
1/2 teaspoon ground nutmeg
1/4 teaspoon grated orange peel
1/2 cup chopped pecans

Preheat oven to 350F (175C). Grease a 9 × 5-inch loaf pan. Beat margarine or butter and sugar in a large bowl until creamy. Beat in eggs and sweet potatoes. Beat in flour, baking soda, baking powder, cinnamon, cloves, nutmeg and orange peel just until moistened. Stir in pecans. Spoon into prepared pan.

Bake 45 to 55 minutes or until a wooden pick inserted in center of loaf comes out clean. Loosen sides of loaf from pan; turn out onto a cooling rack. Cool completely before slicing.

MAKES 1 LOAF.

VARIATION

Substitute 1 cup canned mashed sweet potato for fresh baked sweet potatoes.

Apple-Cheese Brunch Loaf

This quick bread tastes wonderful warm or cool, but is easier to cut into slices if it stands at least 10 minutes after baking.

1/2 cup margarine or butter, at room temperature
2/3 cup plus 1 tablespoon sugar
2 eggs
1/2 cup plain yogurt
2 cups all-purpose flour
1/2 teaspoon baking powder
1/4 teaspoon baking soda
1/4 teaspoon salt
1 large apple, peeled, cored and shredded
2 ounces (1/2 cup) Swiss cheese, shredded
1/2 cup chopped almonds, toasted (see Note, page 205)
1/8 teaspoon ground nutmeg

Preheat oven to 350F (175C). Grease a 9 × 5-inch loaf pan. Beat margarine or butter and 2/3 cup sugar in a large bowl until creamy; beat in eggs and yogurt. Beat in flour, baking powder, baking soda and salt just until moistened.

Stir in apple, cheese and almonds. Spoon into greased pan.

Bake 45 to 50 minutes or until a wooden pick inserted in center of loaf comes out clean. Remove from oven.

Combine the 1 tablespoon sugar and nutmeg in a small bowl; sprinkle on top of warm loaf. Let stand 10 minutes. Cut into slices. Serve warm or at room temperature.

MAKES 1 LOAF.

Hawaiian Nut Bread

With this delicious bread, all you need is a mild-flavored spread.

2/3 cup sugar
1/3 cup solid vegetable shortening
2 eggs
1 cup mashed ripe bananas (about 2 medium)
1 (8-oz.) can crushed pineapple, drained
1/2 cup chopped macadamia nuts or pecans

2 cups all-purpose flour
1 teaspoon baking powder
1/2 teaspoon baking soda
1/4 teaspoon salt
Butter or cream cheese, at room temperature

Preheat oven to 350F (175C). Grease a 9 × 5-inch loaf pan. Beat sugar and shortening in a large bowl until fluffy; beat in eggs. Stir in mashed bananas, drained pineapple and nuts.

Combine flour, baking powder, baking soda and salt in a small bowl. Stir flour mixture into banana mixture until smooth. Spoon into prepared pan.

Bake 50 to 60 minutes or until a wooden pick inserted in center of loaf comes out clean. Remove from pan; cool on a wire rack. Wrap airtight in foil or plastic wrap; let stand overnight for easy slicing.

To serve, cut into 1/4- to 1/2-inch-thick slices. Spread with butter or cream cheese. Cut each slice into halves, quarters or fingers.

MAKES 1 LOAF OR 50 TO 80 APPETIZER SERVINGS.

Smoked-Sausage Muffin Cups

Alternating layers of dough and filling stand on end, like the ever-popular butterflake rolls.

1 (8-oz.) package refrigerator crescent rolls
1 tablespoon finely chopped green onion
2 ounces (1/2 cup) Cheddar cheese, shredded
1/4 teaspoon ground sage
2 or 3 drops hot pepper sauce
2 ounces Kielbasa or smoked sausage, cut into 16 thin slices

Preheat oven to 400F (205C). Grease 8 (2 1/2-inch) muffin cups. Unroll crescent-roll dough. Divide dough into 2 rectangles with 4 triangles in each. With fingers, press together perforations. With a large sharp knife, cut each rectangle lengthwise in half; then cut each half into 6 (2-inch) squares, making a total of 24 squares.

Combine green onion, cheese, sage and hot pepper sauce in a small bowl. Place 1 slice of sausage and about 1 tablespoon cheese mixture on each of 8 dough squares. Top each with another square of dough, another slice of sausage and some cheese mixture. Top each with a third square of dough and place each dough stack on end in a greased muffin cup.

Bake 10 minutes or until bread is golden. Remove from oven. Cool about 5 minutes. Loosen muffins from sides of cups; remove from pan. Serve warm.

MAKES 8 MUFFINS.

Canadian-Bacon Focaccia Strips

Take a baking shortcut by starting with refrigerated or frozen dough.

1 (11-oz.) package refrigerated or frozen French bread dough
2 tablespoons vegetable or olive oil
1 medium onion, chopped
1 clove garlic, crushed
1/4 cup chopped fresh basil
2 tablespoons chopped fresh thyme
6 to 8 slices (about 4 ounces) Canadian bacon, chopped
1 cup (4 ounces) shredded Swiss cheese

Preheat oven to 425F (220C). Lightly grease a 15 × 10-inch shallow baking pan. Pat dough evenly into prepared pan; set aside.

Heat oil in a medium skillet over medium heat. Add onion, garlic, basil and thyme. Cook, stirring occasionally, 10 minutes or until onion is translucent. Spread mixture over top of dough. Sprinkle with bacon, then cheese.

Bake about 20 minutes or until cheese melts and dough is golden brown. Cut into strips.

MAKES 20 TO 25 STRIPS.

Onion-Roquefort Roast Beef Pick-Ups

We use French rolls about six inches long. For smaller servings, try the smaller pillow-shaped rolls.

1 medium red onion, thinly sliced	1 clove garlic, crushed
4 ounces (about 1/2 cup) Roquefort cheese, crumbled	1 tablespoon steak sauce
	1/4 teaspoon salt
1/4 cup olive oil or vegetable oil	1/8 teaspoon pepper
2 tablespoons red-wine vinegar	8 ounces thinly sliced roast beef
1 teaspoon chopped chives	3 large (6-inch) French rolls, split
1 tablespoon chopped fresh parsley	

Separate onion rings; place in a shallow glass container. Sprinkle with Roquefort cheese. Whisk together oil, vinegar, chives, parsley, garlic, steak sauce, salt and pepper in a small bowl. Pour mixture over onions and cheese; toss to coat. Cover and refrigerate at least 2 hours.

At serving time, drain onions and cheese; save marinade. Drape equal amounts of roast beef over each half of French rolls. Top with drained onions and cheese. Spoon additional marinade over top, if desired.

MAKES 6 OPEN-FACE SERVINGS.

Roast Pork and Apple Pizza

Boboli is an Italian-type bread that's often used as a prepared base for pizza. We enjoy using it for this roast pork combination.

1 tablespoon vegetable oil
1 small onion, thinly sliced
1 teaspoon Dijon mustard
1/2 teaspoon grated gingerroot
1 tablespoon fresh orange juice
1/2 teaspoon grated orange peel
1/2 teaspoon chili powder

1 teaspoon brown sugar
1/8 teaspoon salt
1 medium apple, thinly sliced
6 to 8 ounces thinly sliced roast pork
1 (8-oz.) package pizza shells
    (2 [6-inch] shells), warmed

Heat oil in a 10-inch skillet over medium heat. Add onion and cook until onion is limp, about 5 minutes. Stir together mustard, ginger, orange juice, orange peel, chili powder, brown sugar and salt. Add apple and mustard mixture to onion. Cover and cook over low heat until apple is soft, about 5 minutes, stirring occasionally. Add pork; cook until heated.

Spoon half of cooked mixture onto each bread shell. Cut into quarters for ease in eating.

MAKES 2 MAIN-DISH SERVINGS OR 4 SNACK-SIZE SERVINGS.

Open-Face Brie and Leek Flatbread

Similar to a pizza, the quick-and-easy crust is made from a mix. Cut into larger servings to serve as a main dish for lunch.

2 cups buttermilk baking mix
1 teaspoon dried dill weed
10 tablespoons margarine or butter, at room temperature
1/4 cup boiling water
4 medium leeks, thinly sliced
1/8 teaspoon pepper
4 ounces (1 cup) Brie cheese, chopped
4 ounces (1 cup) Swiss cheese, shredded
1/4 cup pine nuts
Cherry tomatoes, quartered, for garnish

Preheat oven to 425F (220C). Mix together baking mix, dill weed and 8 tablespoons of the margarine or butter in a medium bowl. Pour in boiling water, stirring until well blended. Press dough into a 15 × 10-inch jelly-roll pan.

Bake 10 minutes or until light-golden brown. Remove from oven. Reduce oven temperature to 375F (190C).

Meanwhile, melt remaining 2 tablespoons margarine or butter in a large skillet. Add leeks and pepper; cook over medium heat until limp, about 10 minutes.

Spoon leek mixture over baked crust. Top with Brie cheese, Swiss cheese and pine nuts. Bake 5 to 7 minutes or until cheese begins to melt. Cut into 1 1/2- to 1 3/4-inch pieces. Garnish with cherry-tomato pieces. Serve warm.

MAKES 40 TO 50 PIECES.

Favorite Aegean Pizza

Start with time-saving refrigerated pizza dough, then top it with this colorful, appetizing mixture.

1 (10-oz.) package refrigerated pizza dough
2 tablespoons vegetable or olive oil
1 medium leek, thinly sliced
1 red bell pepper, sliced
2 tablespoons chopped fresh oregano
1 clove garlic, crushed
2 medium tomatoes, sliced
1/4 cup sliced pitted ripe olives
4 to 6 ounces mild goat cheese, crumbled
1/3 cup pine nuts, toasted (page 205)

Preheat oven to 425F (220C). Press pizza dough into a 12-inch pizza pan or large shallow baking pan. Bake 5 to 8 minutes or until very lightly browned.

Heat oil in a 10-inch skillet over medium heat. Add leek and bell pepper and cook, stirring, until softened, about 5 minutes. Stir in oregano and garlic.

Spoon leek mixture onto warm pizza crust. Top with tomatoes and olives. Sprinkle with goat cheese, then pine nuts. Bake 10 to 12 minutes or until crust is golden. Cut into wedges.

MAKES 1 (12-INCH) PIZZA.

Barbecued Chicken and Corn Pizza

Here's an unusual pizza with a favorite flavor combination of corn, chicken and barbecue sauce. These baby ears of corn fit just right on mini-pizzas.

1 (1/4-oz.) package active dry yeast (about 1 tablespoon)	6 tablespoons bottled barbecue sauce
1 teaspoon sugar	1 (8 3/4-oz.) can baby ears of corn, drained and rinsed
1 cup warm (110F; 45C) water	1/3 cup chopped green bell pepper
1 teaspoon salt	5 ounces (1 1/4 cups) Cheddar cheese, shredded
2 tablespoons vegetable oil	
3 to 3 1/4 cups all-purpose flour	Black pepper (optional)
1 1/2 cups chopped cooked chicken	Cilantro leaves

Dissolve yeast and sugar in warm water in a large bowl. Let stand about 5 minutes or until foamy. Stir in salt, oil and 1 cup of the flour. Beat 2 minutes or until well blended. Stir in 1 1/2 to 2 cups flour or enough additional flour to make a soft dough. Turn out dough onto a lightly floured board. Knead about 1 minute, working in enough flour to make a stiff dough. Clean and grease bowl. Place dough in greased bowl, turning to grease all sides. Cover and let rise in a warm place until doubled in bulk, 40 to 45 minutes.

Preheat oven to 425F (220C). Grease 2 large baking sheets. Combine chicken and barbecue sauce in a small bowl; set aside. Punch down dough; divide dough into 8 equal pieces. Shape each dough piece into a 5-inch circle with a shallow rim on greased baking sheets. Spread equal amounts of chicken and sauce on dough. Arrange corn on top. Sprinkle with bell pepper and cheese. Season with black pepper, if desired.

Bake 18 to 20 minutes or until crust is golden brown. Garnish with cilantro. Serve warm.

MAKES 8 (5-INCH) PIZZAS.

Thin-Crust Pizza

The crust is thin and flaky, so be careful when you cut it.

1 (7.5-oz.) refrigerated single pie crust
1 small zucchini, coarsely shredded
1/2 cup bottled pizza sauce
1/2 cup (about 2 ounces) chopped sliced pepperoni
1 green onion, thinly sliced
1/4 cup finely chopped yellow or green bell pepper
1/2 teaspoon dried Italian seasoning
2 ounces (1/2 cup) Monterey Jack cheese, shredded

Preheat oven to 425F (220C). Roll out pie crust to about a 13-inch circle. Place in a 12- to 13-inch pizza pan. Sprinkle with shredded zucchini.

Combine pizza sauce, pepperoni, onion, bell pepper and seasoning in a small bowl. Spoon over zucchini. Top with cheese. Bake 15 to 20 minutes or until crust is browned. Let cool 5 minutes; cut into wedges.

MAKES 5 OR 6 SERVINGS.

Roquefort-Onion Rolls

Those who think Roquefort dressing is limited to green salads will be amazed at how great it is in this recipe.

1/3 cup refrigerated thick Roquefort cheese dressing or thick blue cheese dressing
4 ounces (1 cup) Monterey Jack cheese, shredded
2 tablespoons finely chopped green onion
2 tablespoons margarine or butter, melted
4 Kaiser rolls or hamburger buns, split

Preheat broiler. Combine dressing, cheese, green onion and margarine or butter in a small bowl. Spread mixture on cut side of roll halves. Place rolls, cut side up, on broiler pan. Broil 4 to 5 inches from heat source for 2 to 3 minutes or until hot and bubbly. Serve warm.

MAKES 8 ROLLS.

Presto-Pesto Bread

For a "hotter" topping, substitute jalapeño chiles for mild green chiles.

1 (8-oz.) unsliced French baguette
1/2 cup (about 2 ounces) freshly grated Parmesan cheese
1/4 cup chopped fresh basil leaves
1/3 cup mayonnaise
2 tablespoons finely chopped canned mild green chiles
1 clove garlic, crushed
1/4 cup pine nuts

Preheat broiler. Cut bread on the diagonal into about 24 slices. Combine cheese, basil, mayonnaise, chiles and garlic in a small bowl. Spread on 1 side of each bread slice. Arrange slices, pesto side up, on a baking sheet and top with nuts. Broil 5 to 6 inches from heat about 2 minutes or until bubbly. Serve hot.

MAKES ABOUT 24 SLICES.

Party French Wedges

A wonderful change from traditional sandwiches, but easier to eat with a knife and fork.

1 (8-oz.) unsliced round sourdough French bread
3 tablespoons Dijon mustard
2 teaspoons prepared horseradish
1 1/2 teaspoons grated gingerroot
3/4 cup plain yogurt
2 tablespoons honey
2 tablespoons chopped fresh parsley
1 hard-cooked egg, finely chopped
1/4 teaspoon seasoned salt
1/8 teaspoon pepper
12 thin slices salami
12 thin slices cooked ham
18 thin slices pepperoni
6 thin slices provolone or other cheese
1/2 cup ripe olive slices

Split bread horizontally into 3 equal rounds. Combine mustard, horseradish, ginger, yogurt, honey, parsley, chopped egg, seasoned salt and pepper in a small bowl. Spread about 2 tablespoons yogurt mixture on cut sides of each slice of bread.

Place bottom slice, cut side up, on a cutting board. Arrange half of salami, ham, pepperoni and provolone on top of slice. Add middle slice and top with remaining salami, ham, pepperoni and provolone. Add top slice. Spoon remaining mustard mixture over outside of loaf. Sprinkle with olives. Cut loaf into 6 wedges.

MAKES 6 SERVINGS.

Neapolitan Slices

Borrowed from Italy, but equally popular throughout other parts of the world.

1 (1-lb.) loaf unsliced Italian or French bread
1 1/2 cups ricotta cheese, drained
1/3 cup chopped sun-dried tomatoes (oil packed)
1/3 cup freshly grated Parmesan cheese
2 tablespoons chopped fresh basil
1/8 teaspoon black pepper
4 slices (about 4 ounces) mozzarella cheese
4 ounces thinly sliced prosciutto, chopped
1 (6-oz.) jar marinated artichoke hearts, drained and chopped
1 green bell pepper, chopped
2 tablespoons sliced green onion

Slice off top of bread about 1 inch from top. Scoop out center, leaving about a 1/2-inch-thick shell. Save bread crumbs for another purpose.

Combine ricotta cheese, tomatoes, Parmesan cheese, basil and black pepper in a small bowl. Spread half of ricotta cheese mixture on bottom of scooped-out bread. Top with mozzarella cheese. Sprinkle with half the chopped prosciutto and all of the artichokes and bell pepper. Top with remaining ricotta cheese mixture, then remaining prosciutto and green onion. Top with lid of bread; cover and refrigerate at least 2 hours. Cut crosswise into 1- to 1 1/2-inch-thick slices.

MAKES 10 TO 12 SERVINGS.

Hot Open-Face Turkey Sandwich

Start with uncooked ground turkey and teriyaki sauce to produce a hearty main-dish sandwich.

1 tablespoon vegetable oil	1/2 cup canned water chestnuts, drained, rinsed and coarsely chopped
1 pound ground turkey	
1 small onion, thinly sliced	
1/4 cup teriyaki sauce	2 large French rolls, halved and toasted
1 tablespoon honey	
1/4 cup ketchup	1 yellow bell pepper, sliced

Heat oil in a 10-inch skillet over medium heat. Add turkey and onion and cook, stirring to break up turkey, until no longer pink, about 5 minutes. Add teriyaki sauce, honey, ketchup and water chestnuts; simmer about 5 minutes to blend flavors. Spoon on cut side of each French roll. Top with bell pepper.

MAKES 4 OPEN-FACE SANDWICHES.

Breads and Sandwiches

Crunchy Open-Face Sesame Fish Sandwiches

Use fillet of sole, sea bass or your favorite fish for these sandwiches.

4 fish fillets (about 4 ounces each and 1/2 inch thick)
1/4 cup all-purpose flour
1 egg, beaten slightly
1/4 teaspoon salt
1/8 teaspoon pepper
1 tablespoon fresh lemon juice
1/4 cup sesame seeds, toasted (see Note, page 109)

2 tablespoons vegetable oil
2 cups shredded red cabbage
1 orange, peeled and diced
2 tablespoons mayonnaise
2 teaspoons prepared horseradish
2 large (about 6-inch) French rolls, halved and toasted

Coat both sides of fish with flour. Combine egg, salt, pepper and lemon juice in a shallow bowl. Dip coated fish into egg mixture, then into sesame seeds.

Heat oil in a large skillet over medium heat. Add fish and cook, turning once, until browned, 6 to 8 minutes.

Combine cabbage, orange, mayonnaise and horseradish in a medium bowl. Spoon cabbage mixture onto cut side of each toasted bun. Top each with 1 cooked fish fillet.

MAKES 4 SERVINGS.

Acapulco Puffs

Avocado slice will begin to discolor if prepared ahead of time. Tossing with lemon juice will prevent discoloration.

6 ounces (1 1/2 cups) Cheddar cheese, shredded	1/2 teaspoon Dijon mustard
1/3 cup mayonnaise	1/2 teaspoon Worcestershire sauce
1 egg, beaten slightly	4 slices bacon, cooked and crumbled
1 tablespoon finely chopped green onion	1 large tomato, cut into 8 thin slices
2 tablespoons canned diced mild green chiles	4 sourdough English muffins, split and toasted
	1 avocado, cut into 8 thin slices

Preheat oven to 350F (175C). Combine cheese, mayonnaise, egg, green onion, chiles, mustard, Worcestershire sauce and bacon in a small bowl.

Place a tomato slice on each muffin half. Top each with about 2 1/2 tablespoons cheese mixture. Place muffins on a baking sheet. Bake 10 to 15 minutes or until golden and puffy. Top each muffin with an avocado slice. Serve warm.

MAKES 8 SERVINGS.

Crispy Snack Rounds

These are an ideal accompaniment to a green or main-dish salad. Reuse baking sheets as needed until all rounds are baked.

2 cups all-purpose flour
1 cup whole-wheat flour
1/2 teaspoon baking soda
2 tablespoons sugar

1/2 cup solid vegetable shortening
1 cup plain yogurt
1/2 teaspoon dried dill weed
1 1/2 teaspoons coarse salt

Stir together flours, baking soda and sugar in a medium bowl. Cut in shortening until mixture is crumbly. Stir in yogurt and dill weed to make a smooth dough. Cover and refrigerate until chilled.

Preheat oven to 350F (175C). Divide dough into 6 equal pieces and cut each piece into 4 equal pieces, making 24 pieces. Roll each piece into a circle about 6 to 7 inches in diameter.

Place about 2 or 3 circles on each ungreased baking sheet. Sprinkle with coarse salt. Bake 12 to 15 minutes or until golden brown and crisp. Transfer to a wire rack. Repeat with remaining rounds.

MAKES 24 ROUNDS.

Barbecued Beef on a Bun

To make this recipe crunchier, top barbecued beef with a thin layer of shredded cabbage or a slice of sweet onion.

2 pounds beef stew cubes or beef chuck roast, cut into 1-inch cubes
1 small onion, diced
1 cup ketchup
2 tablespoons light brown sugar
1 teaspoon dry mustard
2 tablespoons Worcestershire sauce
1/2 cup beef stock or bouillon
1/4 teaspoon salt
1/8 teaspoon pepper
10 Kaiser rolls or onion rolls, split and warmed

Combine beef with remaining ingredients except rolls in a 4-quart Dutch oven. Cover and simmer over low heat 2 1/2 to 3 hours or until beef is very tender, stirring occasionally.

Transfer warm beef mixture to a food processor. Process briefly to shred. Spoon about 1/2 cup beef and sauce onto each roll. Serve hot.

MAKES 10 SERVINGS.

Open-Face Mini-Reubens

A classic sandwich combination that's spicy enough to be appealing. Serve on small rolls for easy handling.

4 small round French rolls, split	2 teaspoons prepared mustard
2 tablespoons margarine or butter, at room temperature	16 thin slices cooked corned beef or pastrami
8 slices Swiss cheese, halved	1/4 cup mayonnaise
1 cup sauerkraut, well drained	1 tablespoon chili sauce

Preheat broiler. Lightly spread cut sides of rolls with margarine or butter. Arrange half of the Swiss cheese on rolls. Top with sauerkraut, mustard and corned beef or pastrami.

Combine mayonnaise and chili sauce in a small bowl; spoon over meat. Top with remaining Swiss cheese. Place open-face sandwiches on a baking sheet. Broil until warmed, about 5 minutes. Serve warm.

MAKES 8 SMALL OPEN-FACE SANDWICHES.

Mandarin Stir-Fry in Pita Bread

After you slice off the top of a pita bread, insert that piece in the bottom of the pocket to be filled—this prevents the bottom from splitting and leaking.

2 tablespoons vegetable oil
2 teaspoons sesame oil
1 1/3 cups raw small shrimp, peeled and halved
24 snow peas, halved
1/4 cup sliced green onions
1/2 cup sliced canned water chestnuts
1 1/2 tablespoons soy sauce
1 teaspoon grated gingerroot
4 (6-inch) pita bread rounds, warmed
Fresh herbs (optional)

Heat vegetable oil and sesame oil in a small skillet over medium-high heat. Add shrimp; sauté about 1 minute. Stir in snow peas, green onions, water chestnuts, soy sauce and ginger; cook 1 minute.

Slice off top of each pita round. Place top inside bottom to reinforce it. Spoon shrimp mixture into warm pita rounds. Garnish with fresh herbs, if desired. Serve warm.

MAKES 4 SERVINGS.

Vegetable and Cheese-Stuffed Pitas

A salad in a pocket that you can pick up and eat.

3 (8-inch) pita bread rounds, cut in half crosswise
1 (8-oz.) package cream cheese, at room temperature
1 small cucumber, cut into 36 thin slices
Black pepper
1 medium green bell pepper, cut into 36 slivers
6 large leaves romaine lettuce
1/4 cup thinly sliced green onions
1 1/2 ounces (6 tablespoons) blue cheese, crumbled

Carefully open pita bread halves; spread about 2 tablespoons cream cheese inside each pita half. Place 6 cucumber slices in each pita half. Sprinkle generously with black pepper. Top cucumbers with 6 bell pepper slivers and a lettuce leaf. Sprinkle filling with green onions and blue cheese.

MAKES 6 SANDWICHES.

Cashew Chicken Pitas

An enticing combination of flavors provides a Southeast Asian accent.

1 pound boneless, skinless chicken breasts (about 4 halves)
2 tablespoons vegetable oil
1 tablespoon cornstarch
1/3 cup chicken bouillon or broth
2 tablespoons soy sauce
1 tablespoon Dijon mustard
1 tablespoon finely chopped crystallized ginger
1 cup snow peas
1/2 cup sliced canned water chestnuts
3 pita breads, cut in half crosswise
2 tablespoons chopped cashews
2 tangerines, peeled, sectioned and cut into chunks

Cut chicken breasts into about 2 × 1/2-inch strips. Heat oil in a 10-inch skillet over medium heat. Add chicken; cook, stirring, 3 to 4 minutes or until chicken is no longer pink.

Combine cornstarch, chicken broth, soy sauce and mustard in a small bowl; stir into chicken in pan. Cook, stirring, until thickened. Stir in ginger, snow peas and water chestnuts; cook until bubbly. Spoon about 1/2 cup mixture into each pita bread half. Sprinkle with cashews. Top with tangerine chunks.

MAKES 6 SANDWICHES.

Vegetable-Stuffed Pita Rounds

If the smaller Japanese eggplant isn't available, use half of a medium globe eggplant.

2 tablespoons vegetable oil
1 small onion, chopped
1 clove garlic, crushed
2 Japanese eggplants (about 4 ounces each), julienned
1 medium carrot, peeled and thinly sliced
1/4 teaspoon salt
1/2 cup green chile salsa
2 pita bread rounds
1 ounce (1/4 cup) Cheddar cheese, shredded

Preheat oven to 375F (190C). Heat oil in a 10-inch skillet over medium heat. Add onion, garlic, eggplant, carrot and salt. Cook, stirring, until almost tender, about 10 minutes. Add salsa; cook and stir until vegetables are tender.

Halve pita bread crosswise to form 4 pockets. Spoon vegetable mixture into bottom of each pita pocket. Sprinkle with cheese. Wrap in foil. Bake about 10 minutes or until hot.

MAKES 4 SANDWICHES.

Grilled Peanut Butter and Jelly Sandwiches

For a spicy flavor variation, substitute 6 tablespoons room-temperature cream cheese for peanut butter and 1/4 cup jalapeño jelly for grape jelly.

8 slices bread
1/4 cup peanut butter
1/4 cup grape or strawberry
  jelly or jam
3 eggs

2 tablespoons milk
1/4 teaspoon salt
1/8 teaspoon pepper
1 to 2 tablespoons vegetable oil

Spread peanut butter on 1 side of 4 slices of bread. Top with jelly or jam, then remaining slices of bread. Beat eggs, milk, salt and pepper in a medium bowl. Dip sandwiches into egg mixture.

Heat oil in a skillet or griddle over medium heat. Add sandwiches. Cook until browned, turn and brown other side. Cut into halves or quarters.

MAKES 4 SANDWICHES.

Rich Pastry

Freeze the baked shells to use at a later time.

3 1/2 cups all-purpose flour
1/4 teaspoon salt
1 cup (8 ounces) butter, chilled

1 egg
1/4 cup vegetable oil
1/2 cup cold water

Combine flour and salt in a food processor; add butter. Process until mixture resembles oatmeal. Beat egg in a small bowl and stir in oil and water. Add egg mixture to flour mixture; process until dough just forms a ball. Divide dough in half; shape into 2 balls. Wrap in plastic wrap or foil. Refrigerate at least 1 hour.

Preheat oven to 400F (205C). To make 8- or 9-inch pie shells: Roll out 1 ball of dough at a time on a lightly floured surface to a 10-inch circle. Fit into an 8- or 9-inch pie plate without stretching dough. Trim edge 1/2 inch larger than pie plate. Flute edge; prick bottom and side with tines of a fork. Repeat with remaining dough.

To make tart shells: Roll out dough as directed above. Use a 3-inch pastry cutter, top of a jar, bowl or drinking glass to cut dough into 3-inch circles. Carefully fit into 2-inch tart pans or muffin cups without stretching dough. Trim edges even with top of pans or cups. Prick side and bottom of each with tines of a fork.

Bake pastry 10 to 12 minutes or until golden brown. Unbaked shells can be filled with your favorite filling and baked according to that recipe's directions.

MAKES 2 (8- OR 9-INCH) PASTRY SHELLS OR ABOUT 40 TART SHELLS.

Herbed Party Sandwiches

Get out your fancy cutters for party shapes. Arrange finished open-face sandwiches on your prettiest serving tray.

1 1/2 tablespoons chopped fresh tarragon
1 1/2 tablespoons chopped fresh chives
1/4 cup chopped watercress
1 1/2 tablespoons chopped fresh dill
1 cup mayonnaise
30 to 40 thin slices pumpernickel bread
15 to 20 small cooked, peeled shrimp
Fresh dill sprigs, for garnish
15 to 20 small slices cooked chicken
Fresh tarragon sprigs, for garnish
Red bell pepper strips, for garnish (optional)

Combine tarragon, chives, watercress, dill and mayonnaise in a food processor. Process until herbs are finely chopped and blended with mayonnaise.

Cut bread into small hearts, diamonds, rounds or a shape that fits the occasion. Spread each bread shape with 1/2 to 1 teaspoon herbed mayonnaise. Halve shrimp lengthwise, starting along back. Arrange 2 halves, cut side down, on 15 to 20 open-face sandwiches. Garnish with fresh dill.

Arrange 1 chicken slice and a small sprig of fresh tarragon on each of remaining sandwiches. Garnish with bell pepper strips, if desired.

MAKES 30 TO 40 OPEN-FACE SANDWICHES.

Breads and Sandwiches

Sandwich Spreads

Plan on 1/2 cup plain or flavored spread for 45 to 50 open-face sandwiches.

MUSTARD

Combine 1 tablespoon prepared mustard and 1/2 cup softened margarine or butter.

CHIVE

Combine 1 tablespoon minced fresh chives and 1/2 cup softened margarine or butter.

HERB

Combine 1/4 teaspoon crushed dried rosemary leaves, 1/4 teaspoon crushed dried basil leaves, 1/8 teaspoon crushed dried thyme leaves and 1/2 cup softened margarine or butter.

DILL

Combine 1 teaspoon dried dill weed and 1/2 cup softened margarine or butter.

ITALIAN

Combine 1/2 teaspoon crushed dried oregano leaves, 1/2 teaspoon crushed dried basil leaves, 1/2 teaspoon garlic salt and 1/2 cup softened margarine or butter.

ANCHOVY

Combine 2 teaspoons anchovy paste, 1/2 teaspoon lemon juice and 1/2 cup mayonnaise.

RÉMOULADE

Combine 1 tablespoon chopped capers, 1 tablespoon minced fresh chives, 1 teaspoon dried oregano leaves and 1/2 cup mayonnaise.

Cheese

Combine 1/4 cup freshly grated Parmesan cheese or 2 tablespoons crumbled Roquefort cheese, 1 teaspoon chopped fresh parsley and 1/2 cup mayonnaise or sour cream.

Watercress

Combine 1/4 cup minced watercress leaves, 1 tablespoon minced fresh chives and 1/2 cup sour cream.

Parsley and Pimiento

Combine 2 tablespoons chopped fresh parsley, 2 tablespoons chopped pimiento and 1/2 cup softened margarine or butter.

Egg Filling

Egg fillings stretch your budget when making party sandwiches.

4 hard-cooked eggs, chopped
1/4 cup mayonnaise
1/2 teaspoon prepared mustard
1/4 teaspoon salt
1/8 teaspoon pepper

Combine eggs, mayonnaise, mustard, salt and pepper in a small bowl. Cover and refrigerate up to 8 hours if making ahead.

MAKES ABOUT 1 CUP.

VARIATIONS

Add one or more of the following:

2 slices crisp-cooked bacon, crumbled
1/4 cup finely chopped cooked ham and 1 teaspoon drained sweet pickle relish
1/2 teaspoon dried dill weed, crushed, and 1 teaspoon freshly minced chives
1/4 cup finely chopped ripe olives, drained

Tuna Filling

Tuna sandwiches are a favorite of any age group.

1 (6 1/2-oz.) can tuna, drained and flaked
1/3 cup mayonnaise
1/4 cup minced celery
1 tablespoon finely chopped sweet pickle

Combine tuna, mayonnaise, celery and pickle in a small bowl. Cover and refrigerate up to 8 hours if making ahead.

MAKES ABOUT 1 1/4 CUPS.

Breads and Sandwiches

Chicken or Turkey Filling

Fill puffs or fancy sandwiches with this mixture. Serve them at receptions or open houses.

Use a food grinder or a food processor to grind the chicken or turkey.

2 cups cooked ground chicken or turkey
1/4 cup finely chopped celery
1/3 cup mayonnaise
1/8 teaspoon salt
Pinch of pepper

Combine chicken, celery, mayonnaise, salt and pepper in a small bowl. Cover and refrigerate up to 8 hours if making ahead.

MAKES ABOUT 1 1/2 CUPS.

VARIATIONS

Add one or more of the following:

- 1/4 cup chopped toasted almonds or pecans
- 1 tablespoon drained sweet pickle relish and 1/2 teaspoon dried minced onion
- 1 hard-cooked egg, chopped, and 1/2 teaspoon prepared mustard
- 1/4 cup drained, crushed pineapple and 1 tablespoon finely chopped macadamia nuts
- 1/4 cup chopped canned water chestnuts and 1 teaspoon soy sauce

Cream Cheese Filling

For a mild-flavored spread, use only the cheese and milk, or add one or more of the ingredients below (see Variations).

1 (3-oz.) package cream cheese, at room temperature

1 tablespoon milk

Mix together cream cheese and milk in a small bowl until smooth.

MAKES 1/3 CUP.

VARIATIONS

Add one or more of the following:

- 1 tablespoon minced fresh chives and 1 tablespoon minced pimiento
- 2 tablespoons chopped walnuts or pecans
- 2 tablespoons chopped dates or raisins
- 1/4 cup chopped ripe or stuffed green olives, drained
- 2 tablespoons crumbled cooked bacon
- 1 tablespoon finely chopped chutney
- 2 tablespoons finely chopped watercress leaves
- 2 tablespoons crumbled blue cheese

Ham Filling

Ham is a favorite filling for large and small sandwiches. Use a food grinder or a food processor to grind the ham.

2 cups cooked ground ham
1/3 cup mayonnaise
1 teaspoon prepared mustard

1 tablespoon drained sweet pickle relish

Combine ham, mayonnaise, mustard and relish in a small bowl. Cover and refrigerate up to 8 hours if making ahead.

MAKES 1 1/2 CUPS.

VARIATIONS

Add one or more of the following:

1 hard-cooked egg, chopped
1 ounce (1/4 cup) Cheddar cheese, shredded

1 green onion, finely chopped
2 tablespoons minced green bell pepper

Crab and Swiss on Sourdough

When using frozen crabmeat, allow time for thawing, preferably in the refrigerator.

1 (6-oz.) can crabmeat or 1 (6-oz.) package frozen crabmeat
4 ounces (1 cup) Swiss cheese, grated
1/2 cup mayonnaise
2 tablespoons minced green onion
1 tablespoon fresh lemon juice
1/2 teaspoon Worcestershire sauce
1/4 teaspoon salt
1 (8-oz.) can water chestnuts, drained
2 (6- or 7-inch) sourdough rolls

Preheat oven to 400F (205C). Drain and flake canned crabmeat or thaw, drain and flake frozen crabmeat. Combine flaked crabmeat, cheese, mayonnaise, green onion, lemon juice, Worcestershire sauce and salt in a small bowl and stir until combined.

Slice 10 water chestnuts into thirds; set aside. Finely chop remaining water chestnuts and add to crabmeat mixture.

Cut each sourdough roll crosswise into 10 slices. Spoon about 1 tablespoon crabmeat mixture evenly onto each slice. Top each with 1 slice water chestnut. Arrange on an ungreased baking sheet. Bake 10 to 15 minutes or until bubbly and slightly browned. Serve hot.

MAKES 20 APPETIZERS.

Barbecued Porkburgers with Fresh Papaya Relish

Lean ground pork is an interesting change from the traditional beef burger. The water chestnuts add crunch. Papaya relish tops it off with a fresh fruit flavor.

Fresh Papaya Relish (see opposite)
1 1/4 to 1 1/2 pounds lean
  ground pork
1 egg, beaten slightly
1 (8-oz.) can water chestnuts, drained
  and finely chopped
1/4 cup soft bread crumbs
1 tablespoon soy sauce
1/8 teaspoon pepper
6 pieces leaf lettuce
6 sesame-seed hamburger buns

FRESH PAPAYA RELISH

1 small papaya, peeled, seeded
  and chopped
1 jalapeño chile, seeded and chopped
1/4 cup fresh orange juice
1 tablespoon finely chopped
  green onion
1 teaspoon finely chopped fresh
  cilantro
1/8 teaspoon salt

At least 4 hours before serving time, prepare relish. Cover and refrigerate.

Preheat grill. Combine pork, egg, water chestnuts, bread crumbs, soy sauce and pepper in a medium bowl. Gently shape into 6 (5-inch) patties. Place patties on grill rack 4 to 5 inches from heat. Cook 8 to 10 minutes on first side; turn and cook other side 7 minutes or until no longer pink in center. Remove from heat.

Place a leaf of lettuce on bottom portion of each bun; top each with a cooked burger. With a slotted spoon, top burgers with papaya relish. Place top portion of bun on top. Garnish as desired.

MAKES 6 SERVINGS.

FRESH PAPAYA RELISH

In a small bowl, combine papaya, jalapeño chile, orange juice, green onion, cilantro and salt.

Mediterranean Barbecued Burgers

These hearty burgers are designed to fit on large oval French or Italian rolls. For smaller servings, shape meat into five or six patties and serve on hamburger buns.

1 1/4 to 1 1/2 pounds lean ground beef	1 clove garlic, crushed
1 teaspoon chopped fresh oregano or 1/4 teaspoon dried leaf oregano, crushed	1 tablespoon chopped fresh parsley
	8 pimiento-stuffed green olives, sliced
1/2 teaspoon salt	4 slices mozzarella cheese
1/8 teaspoon pepper	4 (5-inch) Italian or French rolls, split
	1 large tomato, cut into 4 slices

Combine beef, oregano, salt, pepper, garlic and parsley in a medium bowl. Gently shape beef mixture into 4 oval patties about 3 1/2 × 7 inches.

Preheat grill. Place patties on grill rack 4 to 5 inches from heat. Grill 5 minutes; turn and cook other side 5 minutes or until almost done. Arrange 2 sliced olives on top of each patty; then 1 slice of cheese. Heat until cheese melts. Remove patties from heat; place on Italian or French rolls. Top each with a tomato slice.

MAKES 4 SERVINGS.

Dips, Spreads and Pâtés

These dishes are the perfect choices to complete a party menu. Usually easy to prepare, dips, spreads and pâtés can be made ahead and refrigerated overnight, helping to avoid the last-minute rush of party foods that need to be prepared just before serving.

When serving, think of color and texture and use pieces of fruit, crudités and special crackers and bread that complement the flavors of the dish.

Velvety Chicken Liver Pâté

So smooth it melts in your mouth, yet this chicken liver and apple pâté is easy to make.

1/2 cup butter, at room temperature
8 ounces chicken livers, halved
1 small onion, chopped
1 small tart apple, peeled, cored and chopped
1/2 teaspoon salt

1/8 teaspoon pepper
2 tablespoons brandy
2 tablespoons whipping cream
Crackers or Melba toast rounds, to serve

Melt 1/4 cup of the butter in a medium skillet over medium-high heat. Add chicken livers; sauté 2 minutes. Add onion, apple, salt and pepper. Cook, stirring, over medium heat about 5 minutes or until apple softens.

Stir in brandy and cream. Spoon mixture into a blender or food processor. Process 2 to 3 minutes or until smooth. Refrigerate about 1 hour or until completely cooled.

In a medium bowl, beat remaining 1/4 cup butter until fluffy; gradually beat in cooled liver mixture. Spoon into a small crock or bowl. Cover and refrigerate at least 2 hours before serving with crackers or Melba toast rounds.

MAKES 2 CUPS.

Chicken-Almond Spread

Seasoned with herbs and wine, this makes a great topping for crackers or Melba toast.

2 tablespoons margarine or butter
1/2 cup chopped blanched almonds
1 whole chicken breast, cooked
1 tablespoon chopped fresh parsley
1/8 teaspoon salt
1/8 teaspoon pepper

2 teaspoons fines herbes
2 tablespoons vegetable oil
3 tablespoons dry white wine
2 tablespoons whipping cream
Crackers or Melba toast, to serve

Melt margarine or butter in a small skillet over medium heat. Add almonds; sauté about 5 minutes or until golden brown. Set aside to cool.

Remove and discard bones and skin from chicken breast; chop meat. Combine chopped chicken, sautéed almonds, parsley, salt, pepper, fines herbes, oil, wine and cream in a blender or food processor; process until almost smooth. Spoon into a serving dish, cover and chill. Serve on crackers or Melba toast.

MAKES 1 1/4 CUPS.

Poor Man's Pâté

Serve this reasonably priced, country-style pâté with interestingly shaped crackers or slices of French bread.

2 slices bacon, chopped
1 small onion, chopped
1 carrot, peeled and finely chopped
6 chicken thighs
8 ounces ground pork
1 tablespoon chopped fresh parsley

1/4 teaspoon ground ginger
1/8 teaspoon poultry seasoning
1 teaspoon salt
1/4 teaspoon pepper
Pinch ground allspice

Cook bacon, onion and carrot in a medium skillet over medium heat until carrots are crisp-tender, about 5 minutes; set aside.

Remove and discard skin and bones from chicken thighs. Cut meat into 1/2-inch pieces. Add chicken and ground pork to bacon mixture in skillet and sauté until meat is browned, about 10 minutes.

Use a slotted spoon to place meat mixture in a blender or food processor. Spoon about 3 tablespoons drippings from skillet into blender; discard remaining drippings. Add parsley, ginger, poultry seasoning, salt, pepper and allspice to meat mixture. Process until almost smooth.

Pour into a 3-cup crock or bowl. Cover and refrigerate 3 to 4 hours before serving.

MAKES ABOUT 3 CUPS.

Turkey Pâté

This updated version of pâté features turkey instead of traditional meats.

2 slices bacon, chopped
2 green onions, finely chopped
1 carrot, peeled and shredded
1 pound ground turkey
1 egg, beaten slightly
2 tablespoons finely chopped fresh parsley
2 teaspoons finely chopped fresh tarragon
1/2 teaspoon ground ginger
1/2 teaspoon salt
1/4 teaspoon pepper
Crackers, to serve

Preheat oven to 350F (175C). Grease an 8 1/2 × 4 1/2-inch loaf pan; set aside.

Cook bacon until almost done in a 10-inch skillet. Remove from heat and drain off fat. Stir onions, carrot, turkey, egg, parsley, tarragon, ginger, salt and pepper into bacon. Press mixture into prepared pan; cover with foil. Bake 50 or 60 minutes.

Remove pan from oven; cover and chill. Invert on a serving tray. Slice and serve on crackers.

MAKES 1 (8 1/2 × 4 1/2-INCH) LOAF.

Salmon Rémoulade Dip

Reminiscent of old New Orleans, rémoulade is usually served as a sauce for cold fish and shellfish.

1 cup sour cream
1 clove garlic, crushed
1 teaspoon prepared mustard
1 1/2 teaspoons fresh tarragon leaves, crushed
1 tablespoon minced fresh parsley
1 teaspoon fresh lemon juice
1 hard-cooked egg, finely chopped
1 (6-oz.) can salmon, drained and flaked
Raw vegetable sticks and flowerets or potato chips for dipping

Combine sour cream, garlic, mustard, tarragon, parsley and lemon juice in a medium bowl. Stir in egg and salmon. Spoon into a serving bowl. Cover and refrigerate until ready to serve. Serve with variety of raw vegetables or potato chips for dipping.

MAKES 1 2/3 CUPS.

Cream Cheese and Lox Pâté

An updated version of an ever-popular combination, but with more complex flavors. Prepare pâté the night before, refrigerate and it's ready to spread on bagels for breakfast.

1 (8-oz.) package cream cheese with herbs and garlic, at room temperature
1/4 cup plain yogurt
1 tablespoon finely chopped fresh parsley
1/4 teaspoon grated lemon peel
1 tablespoon finely chopped green onion
4 ounces thinly sliced smoked salmon (lox), chopped
1/2 teaspoon Dijon mustard
4 to 6 bagels, sliced

Combine cream cheese and yogurt in a medium bowl. Stir in parsley, lemon peel, green onion, salmon and mustard. Serve immediately or cover and refrigerate overnight. Spread cut side of each bagel with pâté.

MAKES ABOUT 1 1/2 CUPS.

Dips, Spreads and Pâtés

Smoked Albacore Dip

Look for smoked albacore at specialty fish markets or delicatessens.

1 (3-oz.) package cream cheese, at room temperature
1 teaspoon prepared horseradish
2 teaspoons finely chopped fresh dill
1/4 teaspoon grated lemon peel
5 to 6 ounces dry smoked albacore or yellowtail, finely chopped or flaked
1 cup plain yogurt
Corn chips

Combine cream cheese, horseradish, dill and lemon peel in a small bowl. Stir in fish and yogurt. Serve with chips.

MAKES 1 3/4 CUPS.

Hot Crab Dip

Keep warm in a small fondue pot or heatproof dish on a hot tray.

1 (6-oz.) can crabmeat or 1 (6-oz.) package frozen crabmeat
1 (3-oz.) package cream cheese, at room temperature
2 teaspoons fresh lemon juice
1 tablespoon finely chopped parsley
1 teaspoon prepared horseradish
1/4 cup chopped roasted red bell pepper
1/2 cup plain yogurt
French bread, sliced, to serve
Potato chips, to serve

Drain and flake canned crabmeat or thaw, drain and flake frozen crabmeat; set aside.

Combine cream cheese, lemon juice, parsley and horseradish in a medium saucepan over low heat and cook, stirring, until cheese melts. Add bell pepper and flaked crabmeat. Cook, stirring, until bubbly. Stir in yogurt and remove from heat.

Serve warm with slices of French bread or potato chips.

MAKES ABOUT 2 CUPS.

Creamy Crab Dip

Delightfully rich and creamy, this dip is made ahead, making party preparation easy.

1 (6-oz.) can crabmeat or 1 (6-oz.) package frozen crabmeat
1/2 cup sour cream
1/2 cup mayonnaise
1 (3-oz.) package cream cheese, at room temperature
1 teaspoon Worcestershire sauce
1 clove garlic, crushed
1/4 teaspoon seasoned salt
1 tablespoon fresh lemon juice
3 or 4 drops hot pepper sauce
Potato chips or corn chips, for dipping

Drain and flake canned crabmeat or thaw, drain and flake frozen crabmeat; set aside.

Combine sour cream, mayonnaise, cream cheese, Worcestershire sauce, garlic, seasoned salt, lemon juice and hot pepper sauce in a medium bowl and stir until blended. Stir in crabmeat. Refrigerate 3 to 4 hours before serving to blend flavors.

Serve cold with potato chips or corn chips for dipping.

MAKES ABOUT 2 CUPS.

Corned-Beef Pâté

The distinctive flavor of corned beef creates a special pâté. We enjoy its finely chopped texture instead of the smooth mixture often associated with pâté.

- 2 tablespoons coarsely chopped green onion
- 2 tablespoons coarsely chopped parsley
- 3 tablespoons coarsely chopped dill pickle
- 10 ounces (2 cups) cooked lean corned beef, cut into cubes
- 1/4 cup mayonnaise
- 2 tablespoons margarine or butter, melted
- 1 tablespoon coarse-grain mustard
- 1 teaspoon Worcestershire sauce
- Rye bread or crackers, to serve

Lightly grease a 2- to 3-cup gelatin mold with vegetable oil. Combine green onion, parsley and dill pickle in a food processor. Process until finely chopped. Add beef and process until finely chopped. Add mayonnaise, margarine or butter, mustard and Worcestershire sauce; process until combined but not smooth.

Spoon mixture into prepared mold. Cover and refrigerate at least 2 hours. Unmold pâté onto a serving plate; serve as a spread for thinly sliced rye bread or crackers.

MAKES ABOUT 2 CUPS.

Layered Pesto Spread

An impressive two-layer spread, it consists of a green base flavored with basil and an off-white cheese top. For a festive look at holiday time, we sprinkle the top with additional chopped parsley and chives; then add red accents to the tray with clusters of cherry tomatoes.

4 ounces blue cheese, crumbled
4 ounces (1/2 cup) ricotta cheese, drained
2 tablespoons margarine or butter, melted
1/2 cup coarsely chopped fresh basil
1 clove garlic, chopped
1 (8-oz.) package cream cheese, at room temperature
3 tablespoons coarsely chopped fresh parsley
2 tablespoons freshly grated Parmesan cheese
1/3 cup pine nuts
2 tablespoons chopped chives
Crackers or French bread, to serve

Line a 3- or 4-cup mold with plastic wrap. Combine blue cheese, ricotta cheese and margarine or butter in a small bowl. Spoon into lined mold; press lightly with the back of a spoon.

Combine basil, garlic, cream cheese, parsley, Parmesan cheese, pine nuts and chives in a blender or food processor fitted with metal blade. Process until well mixed but not smooth. Spoon over cheese mixture in mold; press lightly. Cover and refrigerate at least 2 hours.

To unmold, invert onto a serving tray; remove plastic wrap. Spread mixture on crackers or French bread.

MAKES ABOUT 3 CUPS.

Peppered Cheese

Seasoned pepper contains black and sweet peppers with a variety of herbs and spices.

8 ounces (2 cups) Monterey Jack cheese, shredded
1 (8-oz.) package cream cheese, at room temperature
1 teaspoon fines herbes
1 teaspoon minced fresh chives
1 teaspoon Worcestershire sauce
1 clove garlic, crushed
2 to 3 tablespoons seasoned pepper
Plain or bacon-flavored crackers, to serve

Combine Monterey Jack cheese, cream cheese, fines herbes, chives, Worcestershire sauce and garlic in a medium bowl. Shape cheese mixture into a 5-inch ball; slightly flatten 1 side.

Cut a 12-inch square of waxed paper. On a flat surface, spread seasoned pepper in an even thick layer on waxed paper. Roll cheese ball in pepper until completely covered. Refrigerate 6 hours or overnight. Cheese ball can be stored in refrigerator several days before serving.

To serve, cut into thin slices; serve on crackers.

MAKES 1 (5-INCH) CHEESE BALL.

Cheese Dunk

Dipping the apples and pears in lemon juice prevents them from turning brown.

2 cups cottage cheese, drained
4 ounces (1 cup) sharp Cheddar cheese, shredded
2 ounces blue cheese, crumbled
3 tablespoons mayonnaise
2 tablespoons prepared horseradish
1 tablespoon prepared mustard
3 green onions, finely chopped
1/4 teaspoon salt
1/8 teaspoon pepper
2 apples, sliced and dipped in lemon juice, to serve
2 pears, sliced and dipped in lemon juice, to serve
Potato chips, to serve

Combine cottage cheese, Cheddar cheese, blue cheese, mayonnaise, horseradish, mustard, onions, salt and pepper in a medium bowl. Spoon into a medium serving bowl. Serve with apples, pears and potato chips for dipping.

MAKES ABOUT 3 CUPS.

Cheddar and Ale Dip

Ale or beer contributes a hearty flavor accent to this cheese dip.

8 ounces (2 cups) extra-sharp Cheddar cheese, shredded
1 (3-oz.) package cream cheese, at room temperature
1/2 cup amber ale or beer
2 teaspoons Worcestershire sauce
1 tablespoon chopped fresh chives
2 teaspoons prepared mustard
Pretzel sticks or bread sticks, to serve

Combine Cheddar cheese, cream cheese, beer, Worcestershire sauce, chives and mustard in a food processor or mixer until almost smooth. Serve with pretzels or bread sticks for dipping.

MAKES 2 CUPS.

Chili con Queso

Equally good as a serve-yourself appetizer or as a home-style family main dish.

8 ounces sharp Cheddar cheese, coarsely chopped
8 ounces sharp processed Cheddar cheese, coarsely chopped
2 fresh or canned mild green chiles, seeded
2 green onions, coarsely chopped
2 medium tomatoes, peeled, seeded and chopped
1 teaspoon Worcestershire sauce
Tortilla or corn chips, to serve

Combine cheeses, chiles and onions in a food processor. Process 5 to 10 seconds or until finely chopped. Spoon into a medium saucepan or chafing dish; stir in tomatoes and Worcestershire sauce. Heat until cheese melts, stirring often. Serve hot in chafing dish, fondue pot or small crockery cooker with tortilla or corn chips.

MAKES ABOUT 3 CUPS.

Chutney-Cheese Spread

Spicy but not overpowering, this is one of our favorites.

4 ounces (1 cup) Cheddar cheese, shredded
3 ounces Neufchâtel cheese, at room temperature
1/4 cup fruit chutney
2 green onions, minced
1/4 teaspoon ground ginger
Sesame crackers, to serve

Combine Cheddar cheese and Neufchâtel cheese in a small bowl. Remove fruit from chutney and finely chop. Add chopped fruit and chutney syrup to cheese mixture. Stir in onions and ginger. Chill 6 hours or overnight to blend flavors. Serve with sesame crackers.

MAKES 1 CUP.

Taste-of-Italy Dip

Toasted pine nuts have an enticing rich flavor. Toast until they are golden in color, but be careful—they burn easily.

1/4 cup pine nuts
1/2 cup ricotta cheese, drained
1/2 cup (about 4 ounces) goat cheese, at room temperature
1 tablespoon chopped fresh basil
1/2 cup bottled picante sauce
Corn chips and/or sliced bell peppers, to serve

Preheat oven to 350F (175C). Spoon pine nuts into a pie pan and bake about 5 to 7 minutes or until golden, stirring at least once; cool.

Combine ricotta cheese, goat cheese, basil and picante sauce in a medium bowl. Spoon into a 2-cup serving dish; sprinkle with toasted pine nuts. Place on a medium tray. Surround with chips and/or bell pepper slices.

MAKES ABOUT 1 1/3 CUPS.

King Kamehameha Spread

An ideal appetizer for any Hawaiian party, use as a spread for small sandwiches or on your favorite crackers.

1 1/4 ounces (about 1/3 cup) blue cheese, crumbled, at room temperature
1 (8-oz.) package Neufchâtel cheese, at room temperature
4 teaspoons finely chopped crystallized ginger
1/4 cup chopped macadamia nuts or almonds, toasted (see Note below)
1 (8-oz.) can crushed pineapple, drained

Stir together blue cheese and cream cheese in a small bowl until smooth. Stir in ginger, nuts and pineapple.

MAKES 1 1/2 CUPS.

NOTE

Preheat oven to 350F (175C). Spread nuts in a 9-inch pie or cake pan. Toast about 5 minutes or until golden. Or toast nuts in a dry skillet over low heat until golden.

Dips, Spreads and Pâtés

Green Goddess Dip

Serve fresh, raw vegetables or corn chips as dippers.

8 flat anchovy fillets, finely chopped
1 (3-oz.) package cream cheese,
　at room temperature
1 cup sour cream
1 clove garlic, minced
1/4 cup finely chopped green onions
1/4 cup minced fresh parsley
1/2 teaspoon dried tarragon leaves,
　crushed
1/4 teaspoon pepper
1 tablespoon vinegar

Stir together anchovies and cream cheese in a small bowl. Stir in remaining ingredients.

MAKES 1 1/2 CUPS.

Stuffed Edam Cheese

The shiny, red-coated cheese shell makes an attractive serving container. Serve with crackers or fresh vegetables.

1 (1-lb.) whole Edam cheese, at room temperature
1/4 cup mayonnaise
2 tablespoons dry white wine
2 teaspoons chopped fresh parsley
2 teaspoons chopped fresh chives
2 ounces Swiss cheese, cut in pieces

Cut a 2 1/2-inch circle from top of Edam cheese. Remove and discard circle of red coating. Scoop out center of cheese, leaving about a 1/4-inch shell; leave coating intact. Place pieces of removed cheese in a food processor or blender. Add mayonnaise, wine, parsley, chives and Swiss cheese. Process until smooth. Spoon about 2/3 of cheese mixture evenly into cheese shell. Refrigerate remaining cheese mixture; use to refill shell.

MAKES ABOUT 1 3/4 CUPS.

Smoky Cheese Log

A quick and easy, savory mixture to keep on hand to serve with crackers or fresh fruit or to stuff celery.

8 ounces (2 cups) sharp Cheddar cheese, shredded
8 ounces (2 cups) Swiss cheese, shredded
1/2 cup mayonnaise
1 teaspoon grated onion

1 clove garlic, crushed
1 teaspoon Worcestershire sauce
1/4 teaspoon celery salt
1/8 teaspoon liquid smoke seasoning
2 to 3 drops hot pepper sauce

Mix together Cheddar cheese and Swiss cheese in a medium bowl. Stir in mayonnaise, then remaining ingredients. Shape into a 9 × 3-inch log; wrap airtight in plastic wrap or foil. Refrigerate 3 to 4 hours to blend flavors.

MAKES 1 CHEESE LOG.

Caviar-Crowned Mold

Use a pedestal cake stand or footed sandwich plate to present this spectacular-looking mold.

1 cup cottage cheese, drained
1 cup sour cream
1 teaspoon fresh lemon juice
1 teaspoon Worcestershire sauce
1/4 teaspoon seasoned salt
1/4 cup chilled dry white wine
1 (1/4-oz.) envelope unflavored gelatin
3 hard-cooked eggs
1 (2-oz.) jar red or black caviar
3 green onions, finely chopped
3 lemon slices
Pumpernickel bread or rye bread, thinly sliced, to serve

Line a 9- or 10-inch quiche pan or springform pan with plastic wrap; set aside. Combine cottage cheese, sour cream, lemon juice, Worcestershire sauce and seasoned salt in a blender or food processor. Process until smooth, 10 to 20 seconds.

Pour wine into a small saucepan and sprinkle gelatin over wine. Let stand 1 minute to soften. Stir over low heat until gelatin dissolves. Gradually stir dissolved gelatin mixture into cottage cheese mixture. Pour into prepared pan. Refrigerate until firm, 4 to 6 hours.

Finely chop hard-cooked eggs; set aside. Invert firmly set mold onto a large round platter; remove pan and plastic wrap. Spoon caviar in a 1-inch ring around outer edge on top of mold. Spoon chopped eggs in a 1 1/2-inch ring inside caviar ring. Cover remaining surface with chopped onions. Garnish center with lemon slices. Serve as spread with pumpernickel bread or rye bread.

MAKES 35 TO 40 APPETIZER SERVINGS.

Sampan Spread

Cut the pita bread into thin wedges and arrange around the bowl of spread.

4 hard-cooked eggs, peeled and chopped
1/4 cup sour cream
1/4 cup mayonnaise
2 teaspoons curry powder
1/4 cup fruit chutney
1/4 cup finely chopped peanuts
Pita bread or pumpernickel bread, to serve

Combine chopped eggs, sour cream, mayonnaise and curry powder in a small bowl. Remove fruit from chutney and finely chop. Add chopped fruit and chutney syrup to egg mixture. Spoon into a small serving bowl. Sprinkle peanuts over top. Serve with pita or pumpernickel bread.

MAKES 1 3/4 CUPS.

Moroccan Dip

Garbanzo beans, also called chick-peas, provide an unusual dip for vegetables.

1 (15-oz.) can garbanzo beans, drained and rinsed
2 tablespoons vegetable oil
1 tablespoon fresh lemon juice
2 tablespoons chopped onion
1/2 teaspoon salt
1 teaspoon Worcestershire sauce
2 tablespoons sesame seeds
2 tablespoons chopped fresh parsley
1 jicama, cut into sticks, to serve
1 carrot, cut into sticks, to serve
4 ounces broccoli, cut into flowerets, to serve

Combine beans, oil, lemon juice and onion in a blender; process until pureed. Add salt, Worcestershire sauce and sesame seeds. Process briefly just to combine. Spoon into a small serving dish; sprinkle with parsley. Serve with jicama sticks, carrot sticks and broccoli flowerets.

MAKES 1 1/2 CUPS.

Ranch-Style Bean Dip

This is similar to a regular bean dip, but with more zip. Leave the seeds in the chile if you want it hotter.

1/4 cup margarine or butter	1 (16-oz.) can pinto beans, drained and rinsed
1 small onion, chopped	
1 jalapeño chile, seeded and finely chopped	4 ounces (1 cup) Monterey Jack cheese, shredded
1 clove garlic, crushed	Corn chips, for dipping

Melt margarine or butter in a medium skillet over medium heat. Add onion, jalapeño chile and garlic; sauté, stirring occasionally, until tender, about 5 minutes.

Using a fork, mash beans in a medium bowl. Stir into onion mixture. Cook, stirring, over low heat until hot but not bubbly. Stir in cheese. Cook, stirring, just until cheese melts; do not boil. Spoon into a small fondue pot or small bowl and set on a hot tray. Serve hot with corn chips for dipping.

MAKES ABOUT 2 CUPS.

Pinto Salsa

The dip may be served as soon as it is made or covered and refrigerated overnight.

1 (15-oz.) can pinto beans, drained and rinsed
2 green onions, coarsely chopped
2 plum tomatoes, coarsely chopped
1 jalapeño chile, seeded and chopped
1/4 cup loosely packed fresh cilantro
1 tablespoon vegetable oil
1/2 teaspoon chili powder
1/4 teaspoon ground cumin
1/4 teaspoon salt
Green and yellow squash slices, to serve
Jicama slices, to serve
Radishes, to serve
Corn chips, to serve

Combine beans, green onions, tomatoes, jalapeño chile, cilantro, oil, chili powder, cumin and salt in a blender or food processor. Process until finely chopped, being careful not to puree ingredients. Serve as a dip for vegetables and corn chips.

MAKES ABOUT 2 CUPS.

Eggplant Caviar

Packed with vegetables, this is a wonderful change from the traditional dips and spreads.

2 medium tomatoes
1/4 cup vegetable oil
2 medium onions, finely chopped
1 green bell pepper, finely chopped
1 medium eggplant, peeled and finely chopped

1/2 teaspoon salt
1/4 teaspoon pepper
1 teaspoon sugar
1 teaspoon white-wine vinegar
Toast or crackers, to serve

Peel, seed and finely chop tomatoes. Place in a strainer; let drain about 10 minutes. Heat oil in a large skillet over medium heat. Add onions; sauté 3 minutes or until tender. Stir in green bell pepper and eggplant; sauté 2 to 3 minutes longer. Add drained tomatoes, salt, pepper, sugar and vinegar. Simmer 15 to 20 minutes until vegetables are softened and flavors are blended. Transfer to a bowl, cover and refrigerate at least 2 hours. Serve cold with toast or crackers.

MAKES ABOUT 3 1/2 CUPS.

Eggplant Dip

The unbaked eggplant shell provides a container for the vegetable dip.

1 large eggplant
1 tablespoon fresh lemon juice
1/4 cup olive oil or vegetable oil
1 green bell pepper, diced
2 celery stalks, diced
1 onion, diced
1 carrot, finely chopped
1 clove garlic, crushed
1 tablespoon red-wine vinegar
2 tomatoes, peeled, seeded and chopped
2 tablespoons chopped fresh cilantro leaves
1/4 teaspoon dried basil leaves
1/2 teaspoon salt
1/8 teaspoon cayenne pepper
Pita bread or sourdough bread, to serve

Cut eggplant in half lengthwise. Use a spoon to scoop out pulp, leaving 1/2-inch shells. Reserve pulp. Brush inside of eggplant shells with lemon juice to prevent discoloration; set aside.

Steam or simmer reserved pulp over or in boiling water until tender, about 8 minutes; set aside.

Heat oil in a large skillet over medium heat. Add bell pepper, celery, onion and carrot and sauté 3 to 4 minutes. Stir in garlic, vinegar, tomatoes, cilantro, basil, salt, cayenne pepper and cooked eggplant pulp. Cook, stirring occasionally, over medium heat 10 to 15 minutes or until vegetables are very tender.

Cut pita bread or sourdough bread into wedges; set aside. Spoon cooked vegetable mixture into eggplant shells. Serve warm or refrigerate 1 hour and serve as a dip with pita bread or sourdough bread.

MAKES ABOUT 3 CUPS.

Cheese Caponata

This spicy variation of eggplant caviar with ricotta cheese is excellent cold but even better when served warm.

1/4 cup vegetable oil
1 small eggplant, peeled and diced
2 medium tomatoes, peeled, seeded and diced
1 small onion, diced
1/2 teaspoon salt
1/8 teaspoon pepper
2 tablespoons red-wine vinegar
1 clove garlic, crushed
1 teaspoon prepared mustard
1/4 cup finely chopped ripe olives
1 cup ricotta cheese, drained
French bread, cut or torn into large pieces, or pumpernickel bread, thinly sliced, to serve

Heat oil in a large skillet over medium heat. Add eggplant and sauté 3 to 4 minutes or until limp. Add tomatoes, onion, salt, pepper, vinegar and garlic. Simmer, uncovered, about 5 minutes or until mixture is thick but not dry. Stir in mustard, olives and ricotta cheese. Serve warm or cold. Use as a spread on French bread or pumpernickel bread.

MAKES 3 TO 4 CUPS.

Moussaka Spread

This makes an excellent filling for pita bread.

1 medium eggplant
2 tablespoons olive oil or vegetable oil
5 ounces (1 cup) chopped cooked lamb or beef
1 (6-oz.) can tomato paste
1 clove garlic, crushed
1 tablespoon chopped fresh parsley
1/2 teaspoon salt
1/4 teaspoon pepper
1/8 teaspoon ground nutmeg
1/2 cup plain yogurt
1/4 cup (about 1 ounce) freshly grated Parmesan cheese
Sesame crackers or toasted pita bread, to serve

Preheat oven to 400F (205C). Grease a 3- to 4-cup casserole dish. Prick skin of eggplant several times with a fork. Place punctured eggplant in a shallow 9-inch-square baking pan. Bake about 1 hour or until eggplant collapses. Cool, peel and chop eggplant.

Combine chopped eggplant, oil, lamb or beef, tomato paste, garlic, parsley, salt, pepper and nutmeg in a blender or food processor. Process 5 to 10 seconds or until blended. Mixture will not be smooth. Stir in yogurt. Spoon mixture into greased casserole dish; sprinkle with Parmesan cheese.

Reduce oven heat to 350F (175C). Bake casserole about 30 minutes or until mixture bubbles. To make ahead, refrigerate casserole up to overnight. Bake 35 minutes or until bubbly. Serve hot on sesame crackers or toasted pita bread.

MAKES 3 CUPS.

Garden-Path Dip with Pita Wedges

You'll love this combination of vegetables. For a change, try it with corn chips or tortilla chips.

1 1/2 pounds banana squash
2 tablespoons vegetable oil
1 onion, chopped
1 carrot, peeled and grated
2 celery stalks, chopped
2 small tomatoes, peeled, seeded and chopped
2 tablespoons finely chopped fresh parsley
1 clove garlic, crushed
1 tablespoon white-wine vinegar
2 tablespoons capers
1/2 teaspoon salt
1/4 teaspoon pepper
1/4 teaspoon dried leaf marjoram, crushed
Wedges of pita bread rounds, toasted, to serve

Remove peel from squash; cut squash into 1/2-inch cubes. Heat oil in a large skillet over medium heat. Add squash, onion and carrot; sauté 2 to 3 minutes or until vegetables are softened. Stir in celery, tomatoes, parsley, garlic, vinegar, capers, salt, pepper and marjoram. Cover and cook over medium-low heat 15 to 20 minutes, stirring occasionally. Serve as a dip for toasted wedges of pita bread.

MAKES ABOUT 4 CUPS DIP.

Grace's Salsa

A favorite with our friend, Grace Wheeler. If possible, use fresh Italian plum tomatoes and fresh herbs. If not, use regular vine-ripened tomatoes that are red and flavorful.

Serve with beef, pork, chicken and all kinds of Mexican dishes.

2 medium tomatoes (1 1/2 cups), diced
3 tablespoons minced fresh cilantro
2 small green onions, finely chopped
1 serrano chile, finely minced
3 tablespoons diced canned green chiles

1/2 teaspoon salt
1/8 teaspoon dried oregano leaves, crushed
1/8 teaspoon pepper
3/4 teaspoon cider vinegar

Combine all ingredients in a medium bowl. Serve; refrigerate any leftovers.

MAKES ABOUT 2 CUPS.

Dips, Spreads and Pâtés

Caramelized Onion–Mustard Dip

The flavors are enhanced when this dish is made a day ahead and refrigerated until serving time.

1 tablespoon vegetable oil
2 medium onions, chopped
1 clove garlic, minced
1/4 cup cider vinegar
3 tablespoons honey
1 tablespoon Dijon mustard
1/2 cup low-fat sour cream
1/3 cup plain low-fat yogurt
1/4 teaspoon salt
1/8 teaspoon pepper
Small crackers, sliced yellow or green squash, pea pods or red bell pepper strips, to serve

Heat oil in a large skillet over medium heat. Add onions and garlic. Cover and cook 5 to 10 minutes or until tender. Stir in vinegar and honey. Bring to a boil and cook, uncovered, over medium heat 10 to 15 minutes or until onions are golden and liquid evaporates, stirring occasionally. Cool slightly; stir in remaining ingredients. Cover and refrigerate until chilled. Serve as a dip for crackers or vegetables.

MAKES ABOUT 1 1/3 CUPS DIP.

Jalapeño Pepper Jelly

Do not substitute pectin powder for the liquid pectin in this hot chile and bell pepper jelly.

6 fresh jalapeño chiles, seeded and chopped
1 green bell pepper, chopped
1 cup cider vinegar
4 cups sugar
1 (3-oz.) package or bottle liquid pectin
2 to 3 drops green food coloring (optional)

Sterilize 4 (7- or 8-oz.) jelly jars with screw lids; keep hot. Line a large strainer or colander with 2 layers of cheesecloth; set aside.

Process jalapeño chile, bell pepper and vinegar in a blender or food processor until pureed. Combine pureed pepper mixture and sugar in a 6- or 8-quart saucepan and bring to a full rolling boil over high heat, stirring constantly. Quickly stir in pectin. Bring to a full rolling boil that cannot be stirred down, stirring constantly. Boil hard 1 minute, stirring constantly. Remove from heat; use a metal spoon to skim foam from surface. Stir in green food coloring, if desired.

Strain hot jelly through cheesecloth-lined strainer or colander, pressing mixture with back of spoon to strain out as much pulp as possible. Discard pulp remaining in cheesecloth. Pour liquid into sterile jars and seal.

MAKES 3 2/3 CUPS.

VARIATION

For a milder jelly, substitute 2 fresh mild green chiles for jalapeños.

Yogacado Dip

Avocados and yogurt are a nice combination in this smooth tangy dip, plus the yogurt decreases the amount of fat in each serving of the dip.

2 ripe avocados, peeled, pitted and cut into large pieces
1/2 cup plain yogurt
1/2 teaspoon chili powder
1 teaspoon fresh lemon juice
1 clove garlic, crushed
1/4 teaspoon salt
Variety of raw fresh vegetables or corn chips, for dipping

Combine avocados, yogurt, chili powder, lemon juice, garlic and salt in a blender and process until smooth. Spoon into a small serving bowl. Serve chilled or at room temperature with raw fresh vegetables or corn chips for dipping.

MAKES 1 1/2 CUPS.

Guacamole

You'll get a smoother dip if you process the avocado in your blender, but use a fork to mash if you like it chunkier.

1 large ripe avocado, peeled, pitted and cut into large pieces
2 teaspoons fresh lemon juice
1/4 teaspoon salt
1 canned mild green chile, finely chopped
1/2 teaspoon Worcestershire sauce
1 teaspoon grated onion
3 or 4 drops hot pepper sauce
1 clove garlic, crushed
1 small tomato, chopped
Corn chips or tortilla chips, for dipping

Using a fork, mash avocado in a medium bowl. Stir in lemon juice, salt, green chile, Worcestershire sauce, onion, hot pepper sauce, garlic and tomato. Transfer to a serving bowl. Serve with corn chips or tortilla chips for dipping.

MAKES ABOUT 3/4 CUP.

Dips, Spreads and Pâtés

Microwaved Appetizers and Small Meals

The microwave oven cooks appetizers and small meals in a fraction of the time it takes in a traditional oven.

When microwaving appetizers, arrange larger or thicker foods on the outside edge of the dish, smaller ones in the center. The result will be more even cooking. Also, if your microwave doesn't have a carousel, it's a good idea to stir or rotate the dish a quarter-turn during the cooking process to ensure equal heat penetration.

We cover most appetizers with waxed paper during microwaving to promote even cooking. Remember that food continues to cook after it is removed from the microwave.

The microwave is excellent for heating appetizers that have been made ahead and need warming just before serving.

Green 'n' Gold Vegetable Nachos

If you enjoy hot, spicy foods, sprinkle the nachos with chopped jalapeño chiles just before serving.

2 medium (3 to 4 ounces each) green zucchini
2 medium (3 to 4 ounces each) yellow zucchini or crookneck squash
1 medium tomato, peeled, seeded and chopped
1/3 cup chopped green onions
1 tablespoon chopped fresh cilantro
1/2 teaspoon salt
1/8 teaspoon pepper
4 ounces (1 cup) Jarlsberg or Swiss cheese, shredded

Cut zucchini on diagonal into 1/4-inch-thick slanting slices. Arrange alternate circles of green and yellow squash in a 12-inch-round microwave-safe dish. Cover with waxed paper.

Microwave on 100 percent (HIGH) 3 minutes. Rotate dish 1/4 turn. Microwave on 100 percent (HIGH) 1 minute or until squash is almost fork-tender. Sprinkle chopped tomato, green onions, cilantro, salt, pepper and cheese over cooked squash. Microwave on 70 percent (MEDIUM-HIGH) 3 to 4 minutes or until cheese melts. Serve warm. To eat, pick up individual slices of squash.

MAKES 48 APPETIZERS.

Stuffed New Potatoes

These bite-sized potato boats hold a delicious, spicy filling.

12 small new thin-skinned potatoes (about 1 pound total)
1/3 cup plain yogurt
1/4 teaspoon crushed red pepper flakes
2 teaspoons chopped fresh chives, plus additional for garnish
2 tablespoons minced sun-dried tomatoes (oil packed), drained and patted dry on paper towels

Prick each potato with a fork at least once. Arrange in a circle on a paper-towel-lined, shallow, 10-inch microwave-safe dish. Cover with waxed paper; microwave on 100 percent (HIGH) 3 minutes. Turn potatoes over. Microwave 2 to 3 minutes or until potatoes give slightly when squeezed. Let stand, covered, while preparing filling.

Combine yogurt, pepper, 2 teaspoons chives and tomatoes in a small bowl. Halve potatoes; with a melon baller or teaspoon, scoop out center leaving at least a 1/4-inch-thick shell. Use centers for another purpose, if desired.

Spoon yogurt mixture into the centers of cooked potatoes. Sprinkle with additional chives. Place half of potatoes, filling side up, in a circle on a 10-inch microwave-safe dish. Cover with waxed paper; microwave on 100 percent (HIGH) 1 minute or until heated through. Repeat with remaining potatoes.

MAKES 24 APPETIZERS.

Eggplant Pâté

If you're not a garlic lover, this is wonderful with or without the garlic.

1 medium eggplant (about 1 pound)
2 tablespoons water
1 teaspoon Dijon mustard
1 tablespoon chopped fresh basil or
 1 teaspoon dried basil leaves
2 tablespoons chopped parsley
2 tablespoons plain yogurt
1 clove garlic, chopped
2 tablespoons sun-dried tomatoes
 (oil packed), drained and patted
 dry with paper towels
1/4 teaspoon salt
1/8 teaspoon pepper
1 tablespoon olive oil
Pita bread, cut into thin wedges,
 to serve

Peel and dice eggplant into 1/2-inch cubes. Place eggplant in a 2-quart microwave-safe casserole dish. Sprinkle with water. Cover with waxed paper and microwave on 100 percent (HIGH) 5 minutes. Stir and microwave 4 minutes or until eggplant is fork-tender; drain thoroughly.

Transfer eggplant to a food processor or blender. Add mustard, basil, parsley, yogurt, garlic, tomatoes, salt, pepper and olive oil. Process until almost smooth. Spoon into a small serving bowl. Cover and refrigerate at least 2 hours. Spread on wedges of pita bread.

MAKES ABOUT 1 1/2 CUPS.

Spanish Potato and Onion Tapas

This is our version of a classic tapa *that is served in the bars of Spain.*

3 (5-inch) links hot Italian turkey sausage (8 ounces total)
2 medium (5 to 6 ounces each) baking potatoes, peeled and sliced 1/8 inch thick
1 medium onion, thinly sliced and separated into rings
4 eggs
1/4 teaspoon salt
1/8 teaspoon pepper
2 tablespoons sliced green onion or chopped green bell pepper
1 medium tomato

Remove casings from sausage. Crumble sausage into an 8-inch-round microwave-safe dish. Cover with waxed paper. Microwave at 50 percent (MEDIUM) 2 minutes, stirring after 1 minute (sausage will still be pink). Remove sausage to a bowl.

In the 8-inch round microwave-safe dish, layer potatoes, partially cooked sausage and onion. Cover with waxed paper; microwave on 100 percent (HIGH) 3 minutes; rotate dish 1/4 turn; microwave on 100 percent (HIGH) 3 1/2 minutes or until potatoes are almost fork-tender. Remove dish from oven.

Beat eggs, salt and pepper in a medium bowl; pour over cooked potatoes. Cover with waxed paper; microwave on 50 percent (MEDIUM) 2 minutes. Rotate dish 1/4 turn. Microwave on 100 percent (HIGH) 1 minute. Sprinkle with green onion or bell pepper. Re-cover with waxed paper and let stand 2 minutes. If eggs are not set, microwave on 100 percent (HIGH) for 30-second intervals until done.

Thinly slice tomato and cut each slice in half. To serve, cut into small wedges. Garnish with tomato slices.

MAKES 12 TO 15 WEDGES.

Peppered Artichoke and Salmon Spread

Serve this appetizer in its baking dish or carefully slide it onto a more decorative tray.

2 eggs
2 (6-oz.) jars marinated artichoke hearts, drained
1/3 cup crumbled feta cheese
3 ounces smoked salmon (lox), chopped
1 leek, thinly sliced
1/4 cup chopped red bell pepper, plus additional for garnish
1/2 cup (about 2 ounces) freshly grated Parmesan cheese
Crackers or small wedges of pita bread, to serve

Grease a 9-inch-round microwave-safe casserole dish; set aside. Beat eggs in a medium bowl. Chop artichoke hearts and add to eggs with feta cheese, salmon, leek, 1/4 cup bell pepper and Parmesan cheese; stir to combine. Pour mixture into prepared dish. Cover with waxed paper. Microwave on 70 percent (MEDIUM-HIGH) 5 minutes. Rotate dish 1/4 turn. Microwave on 70 percent (MEDIUM-HIGH) 3 minutes. Let stand, covered, 2 to 3 minutes. Garnish with a ring of chopped red peppers. Spread on crackers or pita bread wedges.

MAKES ABOUT 3 CUPS.

Stuffed Mushrooms Supreme

Sun-dried tomatoes provide a tart, intense tomato flavor; fresh tomatoes would result in a different product.

15 to 20 medium mushrooms (about 3/4 lb.)
1 tablespoon finely chopped ripe olives, drained
2 tablespoons finely chopped sun-dried tomatoes (oil packed), drained and patted dry with paper towels
2 tablespoons crumbled goat cheese
1/8 teaspoon seasoned pepper
2 teaspoons chopped fresh basil or 1/2 teaspoon dried leaf basil
1/8 teaspoon salt
1 teaspoon chopped fresh chives

Wipe mushrooms with a damp cloth; remove and finely chop stems. Combine chopped stems, olives, tomatoes, goat cheese, seasoned pepper, basil, salt and chives in a small bowl. Spoon mixture into mushroom caps. Arrange in a circle on a 10-inch-round microwave-safe dish. If you have more mushrooms than will fit in 1 circle, arrange them in concentric circles.

Cover with waxed paper; microwave on 100 percent (HIGH) 2 minutes. Rotate dish 1/4 turn. Exchange mushrooms on inside of dish with those on outside. Microwave on 100 percent (HIGH) 30 to 60 seconds or until heated through.

MAKES 15 TO 20 APPETIZERS.

Mini-Reuben Rolls

This is a delicious way to use up leftover corned beef. Use either home-cooked corned beef or purchase it from the deli.

7 thin slices (about 4 ounces) cooked corned beef
1 teaspoon prepared mustard
1 1/2 ounces Swiss cheese
1/3 cup sauerkraut, well drained
1 1/2 tablespoons Thousand Island dressing

Cut corned beef slices in half to make 14 strips. Thinly spread 1 side of each strip with mustard. Cut cheese into 14 (1 × 1/2 × 1/4-inch) pieces. Place 1 piece of cheese on each strip of corned beef. Top with about 1 teaspoon sauerkraut and a dab of dressing. Roll up and secure with a wooden pick.

Arrange in a circle in an 8-inch-round microwave-safe dish. Cover with waxed paper and microwave on 100 percent (HIGH) 1 minute or until cheese melts. Let stand 1 minute before serving.

MAKES 14 APPETIZERS.

Peppered Beef Rolls

Serve this beef medium rare; if overcooked to the well-done stage, it becomes tough.

1 pound beef flank steak, trimmed
Sour Cream Sauce (see opposite)
1/4 cup olive oil or vegetable oil
1 cup dry red wine
1 clove garlic, crushed
1/2 teaspoon salt
1/4 teaspoon pepper
6 (7-inch) flour tortillas or pita breads, cut into quarters

SOUR CREAM SAUCE

1/2 cup sour cream
1/4 cup Dijon mustard
2 tablespoons green peppercorns, drained and crushed
2 tablespoons Worcestershire sauce
2 tablespoons chopped fresh chives

Partially freeze steak about 30 minutes to make it easier to slice thinly. Prepare Sour Cream Sauce; cover and refrigerate until needed. Slice steak across grain, into 3/8-inch-thick strips.

Whisk together oil, wine, garlic, salt and pepper in an 8 × 4-inch glass loaf dish. Add steak strips; stir to coat. Cover and refrigerate at least 4 hours or overnight.

Drain steak and discard marinade. Place half of steak strips in a 9-inch-round microwave-safe plate. Cover with waxed paper; microwave on 100 percent (HIGH) 1 1/2 minutes. Stir once, bringing uncooked meat to outside of dish. Microwave on 100 percent (HIGH) 1 minute or until done to your liking. Repeat with remaining meat.

To serve, place 2 strips of steak on a tortilla wedge or pita wedge. Top with a dab of sauce. Roll up and secure with a wooden pick.

MAKES ABOUT 24 APPETIZERS.

SOUR CREAM SAUCE

Mix together all ingredients in a small bowl.

Sweet 'n' Spicy Riblets

If you enjoy a spicier flavor, increase the amount of red pepper flakes.

2 1/2 to 3 pounds pork spareribs, cut in half crosswise
3/4 cup apricot jam
2 tablespoons fresh orange juice
1/2 teaspoon grated orange peel
1/4 cup chunky peanut butter
1/4 teaspoon salt
1/4 teaspoon crushed red pepper flakes

Cut spareribs between bones to form individual riblets; set aside. Combine jam, orange juice, orange peel, peanut butter, salt and pepper flakes in a small bowl; set aside.

Arrange ribs, back side up, in a shallow, 12-inch round microwave-safe dish. Cover with waxed paper; microwave on 100 percent (HIGH) 5 minutes. Exchange uncooked ribs on inside of dish with those on outside. Microwave on 70 percent (MEDIUM-HIGH) 10 minutes. Drain and turn ribs. Brush with sauce. Microwave, uncovered, on 70 percent (MEDIUM-HIGH) 6 minutes. Let stand, covered, 5 minutes before serving.

MAKES 25 TO 30 APPETIZERS.

Pork Spirals

An impressive appetizer, serve it as part of an Asian dinner or with a selection of other appetizers.

4 lean pork chops or cutlets (2 pounds), about 1/2 inch thick	2 tablespoons honey
Salt and pepper	2 tablespoons soy sauce
1 tablespoon Dijon mustard	2 tablespoons hoisin sauce
12 slender green onions, trimmed, plus extra for garnish	1 clove garlic, crushed
	2 tablespoons vegetable oil
	1 teaspoon sesame oil

Remove bones from chops; trim off fat. Place chops 2 inches apart between 2 sheets of plastic wrap or waxed paper. With a meat mallet, lightly pound pork to about 1/8-inch thickness. Sprinkle 1 side of each pork piece with salt and pepper, then spread with mustard. Arrange 3 green onions on long end of mustard-coated side of each pork piece. Cut off green tops from onions to make them the same length as the pork. Roll up; secure with 1 or 2 wooden picks. Place rolls in a 9-inch-square microwave-safe dish.

Combine honey, soy sauce, hoisin sauce, garlic, vegetable oil and sesame oil in a small bowl; pour over pork rolls. Cover and refrigerate at least 2 hours.

Drain pork; reserve marinade. Arrange pork rolls in a microwave-safe dish. Cover with waxed paper; microwave on 50 percent (MEDIUM) 3 1/2 minutes. Exchange uncooked rolls on inside of dish with those on outside. Brush with marinade. Microwave on 50 percent (MEDIUM) 3 minutes or until no longer pink when cut.

Cut each roll crosswise into 8 or 9 slices. Arrange on a serving plate and garnish with green onions.

MAKES 32 TO 36 APPETIZERS.

Chicken-Prosciutto Meatballs

For a change of pace, dip these cooked tidbits in chutney just before serving.

1 pound chicken, skinned, boned and cubed
4 ounces thinly sliced prosciutto, chopped
1 tablespoon chopped fresh parsley
1/4 teaspoon grated orange peel
2 teaspoons chopped fresh chives, plus extra for garnish
1 egg
1/2 cup soft bread crumbs
1/3 cup sour cream
2 teaspoons Worcestershire sauce
1/2 teaspoon salt
1/8 teaspoon pepper
3/4 cup chicken broth or bouillon
1/4 cup white wine
1 teaspoon grated gingerroot

Combine chicken, prosciutto, parsley, orange peel and 2 teaspoons chives in a food processor. Process until chicken is ground. Add egg, bread crumbs, sour cream, Worcestershire sauce, salt and pepper; process until well blended. Form into about 55 (1-inch) balls.

Combine broth, wine and ginger in a 10-inch-round microwave-safe casserole dish. Cover with waxed paper; microwave on 100 percent (HIGH) 1 minute or until boiling. Add half of the meatballs; re-cover with waxed paper. Microwave on 100 percent (HIGH) 2 minutes. Rotate dish 1/4 turn; microwave on 100 percent (HIGH) 30 seconds or until meatballs are no longer pink when cut.

With a slotted spoon, remove meatballs from liquid to a serving bowl; cover to keep warm. Repeat with remaining meatballs. Just before serving, sprinkle with chives; serve warm.

MAKES ABOUT 55 MEATBALLS.

Raspberry-Orange Turkey Kabobs

Check your meat department for the various cuts of turkey that are now available.

1/2 cup fresh or frozen unsweetened raspberries
1/2 cup chicken broth or bouillon
1/2 cup (2 ounces) toasted, skinned hazelnuts (see Note, below)
1/2 teaspoon salt
1/4 teaspoon pepper
1 pound uncooked turkey, boned, skinned and cut into 1-inch cubes
1 tablespoon black raspberry liqueur
2 tablespoons sour cream
2 oranges, peeled and cut into bite-size pieces

Combine raspberries, broth, hazelnuts, salt and pepper in a food processor or blender. Process until nuts are finely chopped.

Arrange turkey cubes in a shallow 9-inch-round microwave-safe dish. Pour raspberry mixture over turkey; stir to coat. Cover with waxed paper; microwave on 70 percent (MEDIUM-HIGH) 3 minutes. Stir, re-cover and microwave on 100 percent (HIGH) 2 minutes. Let stand 1 minute; turkey should no longer be pink when cut. If turkey needs further cooking, microwave on 100 percent (HIGH) for 30-second intervals until done.

With a slotted spoon, remove turkey pieces from dish. Stir liqueur and sour cream into raspberry mixture; then pour into a serving dish.

Thread 1 cooked turkey cube and 1 orange piece on small wooden skewers and place on a serving tray. Let each guest dip kabobs into warm sauce.

MAKES 20 TO 25 APPETIZERS.

NOTE

Toast hazelnuts according to Note on page 205. Rub warm nuts in a heavy towel to remove skins.

Sicilian Stuffed Sole

This is a mini version of a traditional main dish served throughout Sicily.

6 (1/4-inch-thick) fillets of sole or other thin fish fillets (1 pound total)
1 1/2 cups dry bread crumbs
1/4 cup pine nuts, toasted (page 205) and chopped
1/4 cup golden raisins, chopped
1 egg, beaten slightly
2 tablespoons fresh orange juice
2 ounces (1/2 cup) mozzarella cheese, shredded
1/2 teaspoon salt
2 tablespoons olive oil or vegetable oil
2 tablespoons freshly grated Parmesan cheese

Halve fillets crosswise to make 12 pieces. Combine 1 cup of the bread crumbs, pine nuts, raisins, egg, orange juice, mozzarella cheese and salt. Place about 2 tablespoons filling in center of each piece of fish, 1/4 inch from edge. Fold each fillet piece in half to cover filling. Secure with 1 or 2 small wooden picks. Brush rolls with oil.

Combine Parmesan cheese and remaining 1/2 cup dry bread crumbs in a shallow bowl. Roll and pat cheese-crumb mixture on outside of fish rolls. Place 6 rolls in spoke fashion on a shallow 8-inch-round microwave-safe dish. Microwave, uncovered, on 100 percent (HIGH) 2 minutes. Rotate each filled roll 1/2 turn. Microwave on 100 percent (HIGH) 2 minutes or until fish barely flakes when prodded with a fork in thickest portion. Remove to a cutting board. Repeat with remaining 6 rolls. Cut each cooked roll, crosswise, into 3 pieces.

MAKES 36 APPETIZERS.

Treasure Island Shrimp

For a taste of the tropics, these appetizers are a winner.

12 ounces (30 to 35) medium raw shrimp
1/2 cup all-purpose flour
1 egg, beaten slightly
1/2 teaspoon curry powder
2 tablespoons chutney syrup without fruit (see Note below)
1 1/4 cups finely chopped flaked coconut
2 tablespoons margarine or butter

Remove shells but keep tails on shrimp. Split each shrimp lengthwise, from top down, almost but not all the way through; devein. Open shrimp to resemble a butterfly shape.

Place flour in a shallow dish. Mix egg with curry powder and chutney syrup. Place coconut in a shallow dish. Dip each shrimp into flour, then into egg mixture, then coat with coconut.

Melt 1 tablespoon margarine or butter on 100 percent (HIGH) in a round shallow 10-inch microwave-safe dish; brush to coat dish. Microwave half of the shrimp at a time in buttered dish on 100 percent (HIGH) 2 1/2 minutes; let stand 1 minute. Shrimp should no longer be opaque when cut. If they need further cooking, microwave on 100 percent (HIGH) for 30-second intervals until done. Remove to a serving platter.

Clean microwave dish. Repeat with remaining margarine or butter and shrimp.

MAKES 30 TO 35 APPETIZERS.

NOTE

To make chutney syrup, place chutney in a strainer over a bowl. Using the back of a spoon, mash chutney against strainer to press out enough syrup to make 2 tablespoons. Return fruit chunks remaining in strainer to chutney container.

Down-Under Marinated Mussels

Our favorites are the jumbo New Zealand green-tipped mussels.

20 to 24 fresh mussels in shells
3/4 cup vegetable oil
1/4 cup white-wine vinegar
2 tablespoons chopped green onion
1 teaspoon chopped fresh tarragon or 1/4 teaspoon dried tarragon leaves
2 tablespoons chopped pimiento, drained
2 teaspoons chopped fresh cilantro
1/4 teaspoon salt
1/8 teaspoon pepper
Fresh tarragon sprigs, for garnish

Scrub mussels and remove beards; rinse in a bowl of cold water. In a shallow 9- or 10-inch microwave-safe casserole with lid, arrange half of mussels in a circle, leaving center open, if possible. Cover and microwave on 100 percent (HIGH) 1 minute. Rotate dish 1/4 turn. Microwave on 100 percent (HIGH) 1 to 2 minutes or until shells open. Remove cooked mussels to a plate as they open to avoid overcooking. Discard any unopened shells. Repeat with remaining mussels. When cool enough to handle, pull mussels from shells; reserve mussels and refrigerate half of shells.

Whisk together oil, vinegar, onion, tarragon, pimiento, cilantro, salt and pepper in a medium bowl. Gently stir in mussels. Cover and chill at least 2 hours.

Drain mussels; place 1 on each chilled half-shell. Arrange shells on a large deep ice-filled tray. Garnish with fresh tarragon sprigs.

MAKES 20 TO 24 APPETIZERS.

Metric Conversion Charts

COMPARISON TO METRIC MEASURE

When You Know	Symbol	Multiply By	To Find	Symbol
teaspoons	tsp.	5.0	milliliters	ml
tablespoons	tbsp.	15.0	milliliters	ml
fluid ounces	fl. oz.	30.0	milliliters	ml
cups	c	0.24	liters	l
pints	pt.	0.47	liters	l
quarts	qt.	0.95	liters	l
ounces	oz.	28.0	grams	g
pounds	lb.	0.45	kilograms	kg
Fahrenheit	F	5/9 (after subtracting 32)	Celsius	C

FAHRENHEIT TO CELSIUS

F	C
200–205	95
220–225	105
245–250	120
275	135
300–305	150
325–330	165
345–350	175
370–375	190
400–405	205
425–430	220
445–450	230
470–475	245
500	260

LIQUID MEASURE TO MILLILITERS

1/4	teaspoon	=	1.25	milliliters
1/2	teaspoon	=	2.5	milliliters
3/4	teaspoon	=	3.75	milliliters
1	teaspoon	=	5.0	milliliters
1-1/4	teaspoons	=	6.25	milliliters
1-1/2	teaspoons	=	7.5	milliliters
1-3/4	teaspoons	=	8.75	milliliters
2	teaspoons	=	10.0	milliliters
1	tablespoon	=	15.0	milliliters
2	tablespoons	=	30.0	milliliters

LIQUID MEASURE TO LITERS

1/4	cup	=	0.06	liters
1/2	cup	=	0.12	liters
3/4	cup	=	0.18	liters
1	cup	=	0.24	liters
1-1/4	cups	=	0.3	liters
1-1/2	cups	=	0.36	liters
2	cups	=	0.48	liters
2-1/2	cups	=	0.6	liters
3	cups	=	0.72	liters
3-1/2	cups	=	0.84	liters
4	cups	=	0.96	liters
4-1/2	cups	=	1.08	liters
5	cups	=	1.2	liters
5-1/2	cups	=	1.32	liters

Index

Acapulco Puffs, 165
Adriatic Antipasto, 139
All Wrapped Up, 105-122
All-American Turkey Meatballs, 8
Almonds
    Almond-Cherry Turkey Cutlets, 82
    Apple-Cheese Brunch Loaf, 149
    Chicken-Almond Spread, 189
    Toasted Almond and Brie Slices, 36
Alpine Cheese Frittata, 100
Anchovies
    Anchovy Eggs, 46
    Green Goddess Dip, 206
Apples
    Apple-Cheese Brunch Loaf, 149
    Cheese Dunk, 200
    Fruited Rice Salad, 131
    Honey-Curried Chicken and Orzo Salad, 124
    Rhineland Mini-Fajitas, 110
    Roast Pork and Apple Pizza, 154
    Velvety Chicken Liver Pâté, 188
Apricot jam
    Sweet 'n' Spicy Riblets, 234
    Turkey Brochettes, 10
Apricot-pineapple jam
    Sunset Ham Balls, 27
Apricots
    Apricot-Cheesecake Muffins, 147
Artichoke bottoms
    Artichoke Plate, 140
    Crab-Stuffed Artichoke Bottoms, 15
    Venetian Crowns, 50
Artichoke hearts
    Adriatic Antipasto, 139
    Monterey Artichoke Bake, 49
    Neapolitan Slices, 162
    Peppered Artichoke and Salmon Spread, 230
Asparagus
    Filo-Asparagus Fingers, 115
Avocados
    Acapulco Puffs, 165
    Guacamole, 223
    Wild West Salad, 135
    Yogacado Dip, 222

Bacon
    Acapulco Puffs, 165
    Bacon and Cheese Eggs, 47
    Bacon and Cheese Polenta Squares, 39
    Bacon Cheesecake, 42
    Beachcomber Quiche, 44
    Canadian-Bacon Focaccia Strips, 152
    Hearty Salmon Chowder, 89
    No-Liver Chutney Rumaki, 28
    Poor Man's Pâté, 190
    Turkey Pâté, 191
    Wild West Salad, 135
Bali Hai-Style Couscous, 130
Bananas
    Curried Scallops and Fruit Kabobs, 19

Hawaiian Nut Bread, 150
Taste-of-the-Tropics Grilled Chicken Burritos, 107
Barbados Black Bean 'n' Rice Turkey Salad, 133
Barbecued Beef on a Bun, 167
Barbecued Chicken 'n' Noodles, 74
Barbecued Chicken and Corn Pizza, 157
Barbecued Porkburgers with Fresh Papaya Relish, 184
Basic Deviled Eggs, 46
Basil
    Hearty Pasta Salad Bowl, 126
    Layered Pesto Spread, 198
    Pasta à la Pesto, 128
    Pesto-Stuffed Cherry Tomatoes, 65
    Pesto-Style Chicken Fajitas, 106
    Presto-Pesto Bread, 160
Beachcomber Quiche, 44
Bean sprouts
    Korean Omelet Wraps, 114
Beans
    Barbados Black Bean 'n' Rice Turkey Salad, 133
    Bean and Goat Cheese Quesadillas, 116
    Dilled Beans and Carrots, 51
    Falafel Taco Wraps, 119
    French-Style Bean Rounds, 53
    Kaleidoscope Bean Toss, 134
    Marinated Garbanzo Beans, 52
    Moroccan Dip, 211
    Pinto Bean and Turkey Chili, 86
    Pinto Salsa, 213
    Ranch-Style Bean Dip, 212
    Shrimp and Black Bean Wraps, 118
    Tortilla-Cheese Stack, 96
    Turkey Tortilla Crisp, 87
    Wild West Salad, 135
Beef
    Barbecued Beef on a Bun, 167
    Beef Yakitori, 31
    Beefy-Mushroom Pinwheels, 34
    Classic Sweet and Sour Meatballs, 32
    Corned-Beef Pâté, 197
    Crunchy Meatballs, 33
    Korean-Style Beef and Mushrooms, 29
    Mediterranean Barbecued Burgers, 185
    Mini-Reuben Rolls, 232
    Onion-Roquefort Roast Beef Pick-Ups, 153
    Open-Face Mini-Reubens, 168
    Peppered Beef Rolls, 233
    Teriyaki Roll-Ups, 30
Beets
    Pickled Eggs and Beets, 48
Bombay Chicken Pinwheels, 3
Bouillabaisse-Style Seafood Bites, 12
Bran cereal
    Topsy-Turvy Maple-Walnut Pumpkin Muffins, 144

Breads and Sandwiches, 143-185
Brie en Croûte, 37
Broccoli
    Moroccan Dip, 211
    Pesto-Style Chicken Fajitas, 106
Broiled Halibut with Tropical Salsa, 88
Brussels sprouts
    Stuffed Brussels Sprouts, 54
Butterflied Bayou Shrimp, 16

Cabbage
    Crunchy Open-Face Sesame Fish Sandwiches, 164
California Quiche, 98
Canadian-Bacon Focaccia Strips, 152
Caramelized Onion-Mustard Dip, 220
Carrots
    Dilled Beans and Carrots, 51
    Eat-with-Your-Hands Italian Salad, 129
    Spiced Carrot Sticks, 55
Cashews
    Cashew Chicken Pitas, 171
Caviar Eggs, 46
Caviar-Crowned Mold, 209
Celery
    Eggplant Dip, 215
    Garden-Path Dip with Pita Wedges, 218
Cheddar and Ale Dip, 201
Cheese
    Acapulco Puffs, 165
    Adriatic Antipasto, 139
    Alpine Cheese Frittata, 100
    Apple-Cheese Brunch Loaf, 149
    Apricot-Cheesecake Muffins, 147
    Bacon and Cheese Polenta Squares, 39
    Bacon Cheesecake, 42
    Beachcomber Quiche, 44
    Bean and Goat Cheese Quesadillas, 116
    Brie en Croûte, 37
    California Quiche, 98
    Canadian-Bacon Focaccia Strips, 152
    Caviar-Crowned Mold, 209
    Cheddar and Ale Dip, 201
    Cheese Caponata, 216
    Cheese Dunk, 200
    Cheese-Stuffed Zucchini, 67
    Chili con Queso, 202
    Chutney-Cheese Spread, 203
    Confetti Polenta Cups, 40
    Crab and Swiss on Sourdough, 183
    Cream Cheese and Lox Pâté, 193
    Cream Cheese Filling, 181
    Creamy Crab Dip, 196
    Deli-Potato Salad Wrap-Ups, 136
    Dilly Cheese Cubes, 38
    Eat-with-Your-Hands Italian Salad, 129
    Favorite Aegean Pizza, 156
    Filo-Asparagus Fingers, 115
    Giant Chicken-Stuffed Shells, 79
    Green 'n' Gold Vegetable Nachos, 226
    Green Goddess Dip, 206

Hearty Pasta Salad Bowl, 126
Hot Crab Dip, 195
Hot Potato Nests, 61
Italian Envelopes, 113
Jalapeño Corn Muffins, 146
King Kamehameha Spread, 205
Layered Pesto Spread, 198
Mediterranean Barbecued Burgers, 185
Mediterranean Sampler, 41
Mexican Pizza, 43
Mini-Reuben Rolls, 232
Monterey Artichoke Bake, 49
Neapolitan Slices, 162
Onion-Roquefort Roast Beef Pick-Ups, 153
Open-Face Brie and Leek Flatbread, 155
Open-Face Mini-Reubens, 168
Parmesan- and Goat-Cheese Potato Wedges, 60
Party French Wedges, 161
Pasta à la Pesto, 128
Peppered Artichoke and Salmon Spread, 230
Peppered Cheese, 199
Peppered Rice Salad with Goat Cheese, 132
Pesto-Stuffed Cherry Tomatoes, 65
Presto-Pesto Bread, 160
Ranch-Style Bean Dip, 212
Risotto Pinwheel Wraps, 121
Roquefort Torta, 97
Roquefort-Onion Rolls, 159
Salmon-Stuffed Tomatoes, 66
Sicilian Stuffed Sole, 238
Smoked Albacore Dip, 194
Smoked-Sausage Muffin Cups, 151
Smoky Cheese Log, 208
Stuffed Brussels Sprouts, 54
Stuffed Mushrooms Supreme, 231
Stuffed Radish Roses, 63
Stuffed Cucumber Slices, 56
Stuffed Edam Cheese, 207
Taste-of-Italy Dip, 204
Thin-Crust Pizza, 158
Toasted Almond and Brie Slices, 36
Tortilla-Cheese Stack, 96
Vegetable and Cheese-Stuffed Pitas, 170
Venetian Crowns, 50
Wild West Salad, 135
Zucchini Appetizer Pie, 68
Zucchini Bites, 69
Zucchini-Cheese Frittata, 101
Cherries
 Almond-Cherry Turkey Cutlets, 82
Chicken
 Barbecued Chicken 'n' Noodles, 74
 Barbecued Chicken and Corn Pizza, 157
 Bombay Chicken Pinwheels, 3
 Cashew Chicken Pitas, 171
 Chicken and Prosciutto Roulades, 78
 Chicken and Water Chestnuts, 80
 Chicken Barrel Roll-Ups, 2
 Chicken Dijon Tidbits, 5
 Chicken or Turkey Filling, 180
 Chicken Saté, 7

Chicken Siam, 73
Chicken-Almond Spread, 189
Chicken-Leek Filo Roll-Ups, 108
Chicken-Mustard Rolls, 81
Chicken-Prosciutto Meatballs, 236
Curried Chicken in Pasta Shells, 76
Giant Chicken-Stuffed Shells, 79
Herb-Grilled Chicken, 72
Honey-Curried Chicken and Orzo Salad, 124
Maple Orange Chicken, 77
Munchy Sesame Wings, 4
Pesto-Style Chicken Fajitas, 106
Poor Man's Pâté, 190
Shangri-La Drumsticks, 75
Tahitian Sunset Roll-Ups, 6
Taste-of-Thai Bowl, 125
Taste-of-the-Tropics Grilled Chicken Burritos, 107
Velvety Chicken Liver Pâté, 188
Chiles
 Acapulco Puffs, 165
 Bacon and Cheese Polenta Squares, 39
 Chili con Queso, 202
 Fresh Papaya Relish, 184
 Fruit Salsa, 107
 Grace's Salsa, 219
 Jalapeño Corn Muffins, 146
 Jalapeño Pepper Jelly, 221
 Jalapeño Pickled Eggs, 45
 Mexican Pizza, 43
 Pinto Salsa, 213
 Ranch-Style Bean Dip, 212
 Sausage and Eggs with Tortilla Strips, 102
 Tortilla-Cheese Stack, 96
Chili con Queso, 202
Chili
 Pinto Bean and Turkey Chili, 86
Chinese Barbecued Riblets, 26
Chinese cabbage
 Taste-of-Thai Bowl, 125
Chowder
 Hearty Salmon Chowder, 89
Chutney-Cheese Spread, 203
Classic Sweet and Sour Meatballs, 32
Coconut
 Curried Chicken in Pasta Shells, 76
 Curried Pork Fold-overs, 112
 Honey-Curried Chicken and Orzo Salad, 124
 Tahitian Sunset Roll-Ups, 6
 Treasure Island Shrimp, 239
Confetti Polenta Cups, 40
Corn
 Bacon and Cheese Polenta Squares, 39
 Barbecued Chicken and Corn Pizza, 157
 Jalapeño Corn Muffins, 146
 Kaleidoscope Bean Toss, 134
 Skewered Szechuan-Style Barbecued Pork, 20
Corned-Beef Pâté, 197
Couscous
 Bali Hai-Style Couscous, 130
Crabmeat
 Artichoke Plate, 140
 Crab and Swiss on Sourdough, 183
 Crab-Stuffed Artichoke Bottoms, 15

Creamy Crab Dip, 196
Hot Crab Dip, 195
Sesame-Crab Dumplings, 14
Cranberry sauce
 All-American Turkey Meatballs, 8
 Easy Barbecued Turkey Cubes, 9
 Orange and Cranberry Turkey Loaf, 83
Creamy Crab Dip, 196
Crispy Snack Rounds, 166
Crunchy Meatballs, 33
Crunchy Open-Face Sesame Fish Sandwiches, 164
Cucumbers
 Falafel Taco Wraps, 119
 Nordic Potato Salad, 137
 Stuffed Cucumber Slices, 56
 Vegetable and Cheese-Stuffed Pitas, 170
Curried Chicken in Pasta Shells, 76
Curried Chutney Eggs, 46
Curried Pork Fold-overs, 112
Curried Scallops and Fruit Kabobs, 19
Curried Sweet Potato Soup, 104

Deli-Potato Salad Wrap-Ups, 136
Dilled Beans and Carrots, 51
Dilled Smoked Salmon Tarts, 90
Dilly Cheese Cubes, 38
Dipping Sauce, 3, 111
Dips, Spreads and Pâtés, 187-223
Dips
 Caramelized Onion-Mustard Dip, 220
 Cheddar and Ale Dip, 201
 Cheese Dunk, 200
 Chili con Queso, 202
 Creamy Crab Dip, 196
 Eggplant Dip, 215
 Garden-Path Dip with Pita Wedges, 218
 Green Goddess Dip, 206
 Guacamole, 223
 Hot Crab Dip, 195
 Moroccan Dip, 211
 Pinto Salsa, 213
 Ranch-Style Bean Dip, 212
 Salmon Remoulade Dip, 192
 Smoked Albacore Dip, 194
 Taste-of-Italy Dip, 204
 Yogacado Dip, 222
Double-Salmon Pinwheels, 13
Down-Under Marinated Mussels, 240

Easy Barbecued Turkey Cubes, 9
Eat-with-Your-Hands Italian Salad, 129
Eggplant
 Cheese Caponata, 216
 Eggplant Caviar, 214
 Eggplant Dip, 215
 Eggplant Pâté, 228
 Moussaka Spread, 217
 Vegetable-Stuffed Pita Rounds, 172
Eggs
 Alpine Cheese Frittata, 100
 Anchovy Eggs, 46
 Artichoke Plate, 140
 Bacon and Cheese Eggs, 47
 Basic Deviled Eggs, 46
 California Quiche, 98
 Caviar Eggs, 46

Index 243

Eggs (cont.)
    Caviar-Crowned Mold, 209
    Curried Chutney Eggs, 46
    Egg Filling, 178
    Fresh Herbed Eggs, 47
    Ham 'n' Egg Wrap 'n' Go, 120
    Jalapeño Pickled Eggs, 45
    Korean Omelet Wraps, 114
    Layered Sausage and Mushroom Omelet, 99
    Parma Eggs, 47
    Party French Wedges, 161
    Pickled Eggs and Beets, 48
    Rosy Eggs, 47
    Sampan Spread, 210
    Sausage and Eggs with Tortilla Strips, 102
    Smoky Deviled Eggs, 47
    Spanish Potato and Onion Tapas, 229
    Zucchini-Cheese Frittata, 101
Falafel Taco Wraps, 119
Favorite Aegean Pizza, 156
Fennel and Oranges with Lemon Vinaigrette, 138
Filo dough
    Chicken-Leek Filo Roll-Ups, 108
    Filo-Asparagus Fingers, 115
    Spinach-Filled Filo Cups, 64
Fish
    Broiled Halibut with Tropical Salsa, 88
    Cream Cheese and Lox Pâté, 193
    Crunchy Open-Face Sesame Fish Sandwiches, 164
    Dilled Smoked Salmon Tarts, 90
    Double-Salmon Pinwheels, 13
    Hearty Salmon Chowder, 89
    Layered Polenta Fish, 11
    Nordic Potato Salad, 137
    Peppered Artichoke and Salmon Spread, 230
    Salmon Remoulade Dip, 192
    Salmon-Stuffed Tomatoes, 66
    Sicilian Stuffed Sole, 238
    Smoked Albacore Dip, 194
    Tuna Filling, 179
French-Style Bean Rounds, 53
Fresh Herbed Eggs, 47
Frittatas
    Alpine Cheese Frittata, 100
    Zucchini-Cheese Frittata, 101
Fruit Salsa, 107
Fruited Rice Salad, 131

Garden-Path Dip with Pita Wedges, 218
Giant Chicken-Stuffed Shells, 79
Gingered Shrimp Balls, 18
Glazed Orange Mustard Ham, 95
Grace's Salsa, 219
Grape leaves
    Stuffed Grape Leaves, 117
Grapes
    Toasted Almond and Brie Slices, 36
Greek-Style Mushrooms, 57
Green 'n' Gold Vegetable Nachos, 226
Green Goddess Dip, 206
Grilled Ginger-Honey Shrimp, 91
Grilled Peanut Butter and Jelly Sandwiches, 173
Guacamole, 223

Ham
    Chicken Barrel Roll-Ups, 2
    Glazed Orange Mustard Ham, 95
    Ham 'n' Egg Wrap 'n' Go, 120
    Hearty Pasta Salad Bowl, 126
    Party French Wedges, 161
    Stuffed Snow Peas, 59
    Sunset Ham Balls, 27
Hawaiian Nut Bread, 150
Hazelnuts
    Raspberry-Orange Turkey Kabobs, 237
Hearty Pasta Salad Bowl, 126
Hearty Salmon Chowder, 89
Herb-Grilled Chicken, 72
Herb-Parmesan Muffins, 145
Herbed Party Sandwiches, 175
Hoisin sauce
    Chinese Barbecued Riblets, 26
    Oriental-Style Baby-Back Ribs, 24
    Skewered Szechuan-Style Barbecued Pork, 20
    Taste-of-Thai Bowl, 125
Hominy
    Multicolored Pozole, 94
    Wild West Salad, 135
Honey Dressing, 124
Honey-Curried Chicken and Orzo Salad, 124
Hot Crab Dip, 195
Hot Open-Face Turkey Sandwich, 163
Hot Potato Nests, 61
Indonesian Pork Saté, 22

Introduction, ix-x
Italian Envelopes, 113

Jalapeño Corn Muffins, 146
Jalapeño Pepper Jelly, 221
Jalapeño Pickled Eggs, 45
Jelly
    Jalapeño Pepper Jelly, 221
Jicama
    Honey-Curried Chicken and Orzo Salad, 124
    Moroccan Dip, 211
    Shiitake Pork Spring Rolls, 111
    Tortilla-Cheese Stack, 96

Kaleidoscope Bean Toss, 134
King Kamehameha Spread, 205
Kiwi fruit
    Broiled Halibut with Tropical Salsa, 88
Korean Omelet Wraps, 114
Korean-Style Beef and Mushrooms, 29

Lamb
    Moussaka Spread, 217
Layered Pesto Spread, 198
Layered Polenta Fish, 11
Layered Sausage and Mushroom Omelet, 99
Leeks
    Double-Squash Cups, 62
    Chicken-Leek Filo Roll-Ups, 108
    Favorite Aegean Pizza, 156
    Hearty Salmon Chowder, 89
    Open-Face Brie and Leek Flatbread, 155
Little Savory Bites, 1-69
Luau Sauce, 23

Macadamia nuts
    Bali Hai-Style Couscous, 130
    Hawaiian Nut Bread, 150
    King Kamehameha Spread, 205
    Spicy Chops with Mango Glaze, 92
Mandarin Stir-Fry in Pita Bread, 169
Mangoes
    Fruit Salsa, 107
    Spicy Chops with Mango Glaze, 92
    Taste-of-Thai Bowl, 125
Maple Orange Chicken, 77
Marinated Garbanzo Beans, 52
Meatballs with Luau Sauce, 23
Mediterranean Barbecued Burgers, 185
Mediterranean Sampler, 41
Mexican Pizza, 43
Mexican Pork Cubes, 21
Microwaved Appetizers and Small Meals, 225-240
Mini-Reuben Rolls, 232
Monterey Artichoke Bake, 49
Moroccan Dip, 211
Mortadella
    Deli Party Carousel, 35
    Eat-with-Your-Hands Italian Salad, 129
    Risotto Pinwheel Wraps, 121
Moussaka Spread, 217
Muffins
    Apricot-Cheesecake Muffins, 147
    Herb-Parmesan Muffins, 145
    Jalapeño Corn Muffins, 146
    Topsy-Turvy Maple-Walnut Pumpkin Muffins, 144
Multicolored Pozole, 94
Munchy Sesame Wings, 4
Mushrooms
    Adriatic Antipasto, 139
    Beefy-Mushroom Pinwheels, 34
    Dilled Smoked Salmon Tarts, 90
    Greek-Style Mushrooms, 57
    Korean-Style Beef and Mushrooms, 29
    Layered Sausage and Mushroom Omelet, 99
    Orange Risotto with Turkey, 85
    Sausage-Stuffed Mushrooms, 58
    Shiitake Pork Spring Rolls, 111
    Spinach-Filled Filo Cups, 64
    Stuffed Mushrooms Supreme, 231
Mussels
    Down-Under Marinated Mussels, 240

Neapolitan Slices, 162
No-Liver Chutney Rumaki, 28
Nordic Potato Salad, 137
Nuts, toasting, 205

Olives
    California Quiche, 98
    Cheese Caponata, 216
    Favorite Aegean Pizza, 156
    Mediterranean Barbecued Burgers, 185
    Party French Wedges, 161
    Stuffed Mushrooms Supreme, 231
    Venetian Crowns, 50
Omelets
    Korean Omelet Wraps, 114
    Layered Sausage and Mushroom Omelet, 99
Onions
    Caramelized Onion-Mustard Dip, 220

244   *Index*

Onion-Roquefort Roast Beef Pick-Ups, 153
Open-Face Brie and Leek Flatbread, 155
Open-Face Mini-Reubens, 168
Orange and Cranberry Turkey Loaf, 83
Orange Risotto with Turkey, 85
Oranges
   Crunchy Open-Face Sesame Fish Sandwiches, 164
   Curried Sweet Potato Soup, 104
   Fennel and Oranges with Lemon Vinaigrette, 138
   Raspberry-Orange Turkey Kabobs, 237
Oriental-Style Baby-Back Ribs, 24

Papayas
   Bali Hai-Style Couscous, 130
   Fresh Papaya Relish, 184
Parma Eggs, 47
Parmesan- and Goat-Cheese Potato Wedges, 60
Party French Wedges, 161
Party sandwiches
   Herbed Party Sandwiches, 175
Pasta
   Alpine Cheese Frittata, 100
   Barbecued Chicken 'n' Noodles, 74
   Curried Chicken in Pasta Shells, 76
   Eat-with-Your-Hands Italian Salad, 129
   Giant Chicken-Stuffed Shells, 79
   Hearty Pasta Salad Bowl, 126
   Honey-Curried Chicken and Orzo Salad, 124
   Pasta à la Pesto, 128
   Sun-Dried Tomato Pasta, 127
Pastrami
   Deli Party Carousel, 35
Pastry
   Rich Pastry, 174
Pâté
   Corned-Beef Pâté, 197
   Cream Cheese and Lox Pâté, 193
   Poor Man's Pâté, 190
   Turkey Pâté, 191
   Velvety Chicken Liver Pâté, 188
Peanut butter
   Chicken Saté, 7
   Dipping Sauce, 3
   Grilled Peanut Butter and Jelly Sandwiches, 173
   Sweet 'n' Spicy Riblets, 234
   Thai Curried Turkey Wraps, 122
Peanuts
   Chicken Siam, 73
   Curried Chicken in Pasta Shells, 76
   Indonesian Pork Saté, 22
   Sampan Spread, 210
Pears
   Cheese Dunk, 200
   Toasted Almond and Brie Slices, 36
Peas
   Cashew Chicken Pitas, 171
   Ham 'n' Egg Wrap 'n' Go, 120
   Mandarin Stir-Fry in Pita Bread, 169
   Stuffed Snow Peas, 59
   Thai Curried Turkey Wraps, 122
Pecans
   Sweet Potato Pecan Bread, 148
Peppered Artichoke and Salmon Spread, 230
Peppered Beef Rolls, 233
Peppered Cheese, 199

Peppered Rice Salad with Goat Cheese, 132
Pepperoni
   Mediterranean Sampler, 41
   Party French Wedges, 161
   Thin-Crust Pizza, 158
   Venetian Crowns, 50
Pesto-Stuffed Cherry Tomatoes, 65
Pesto-Style Chicken Fajitas, 106
Pickled Eggs and Beets, 48
Pickled Shrimp, 17
Pine nuts
   Bacon Cheesecake, 42
   Chicken-Leek Filo Roll-Ups, 108
   Favorite Aegean Pizza, 156
   Fruited Rice Salad, 131
   Giant Chicken-Stuffed Shells, 79
   Layered Pesto Spread, 198
   Open-Face Brie and Leek Flatbread, 155
   Pasta à la Pesto, 128
   Pesto-Style Chicken Fajitas, 106
   Presto-Pesto Bread, 160
   Sicilian Stuffed Sole, 238
   Spinach-Filled Filo Cups, 64
   Stuffed Grape Leaves, 117
   Taste-of-Italy Dip, 204
Pineapple
   Bali Hai-Style Couscous, 130
   Curried Scallops and Fruit Kabobs, 19
   Fruit Salsa, 107
   Hawaiian Nut Bread, 150
   King Kamehameha Spread, 205
   Sweet and Sour Sauce, 32
   Taste-of-Thai Bowl, 125
Pinto Bean and Turkey Chili, 86
Pinto Salsa, 213
Pizza
   Mexican Pizza, 43
   Barbecued Chicken and Corn Pizza, 157
   Favorite Aegean Pizza, 156
   Roast Pork and Apple Pizza, 154
   Thin-Crust Pizza, 158
Plum jelly
   Plum-Glazed Spareribs, 25
Polenta
   Bacon and Cheese Polenta Squares, 39
   Confetti Polenta Cups, 40
   Layered Polenta Fish, 11
Poor Man's Pâté, 190
Pork (see also ham and sausage)
   Barbecued Porkburgers with Fresh Papaya Relish, 184
   Chinese Barbecued Riblets, 26
   Crunchy Meatballs, 33
   Curried Pork Fold-overs, 112
   Indonesian Pork Saté, 22
   Meatballs with Luau Sauce, 23
   Mexican Pork Cubes, 21
   Multicolored Pozole, 94
   Oriental-Style Baby-Back Ribs, 24
   Plum-Glazed Spareribs, 25
   Poor Man's Pâté, 190
   Pork Spirals, 235
   Rhineland Mini-Fajitas, 110
   Roast Pork and Apple Pizza, 154
   Shiitake Pork Spring Rolls, 111
   Skewered Szechuan-Style Barbecued Pork, 20
   South Seas Pork, 93

Spicy Chops with Mango Glaze, 92
Sweet 'n' Spicy Riblets, 234
Potatoes
   Deli-Potato Salad Wrap-Ups, 136
   Hot Potato Nests, 61
   Nordic Potato Salad, 137
   Parmesan- and Goat-Cheese Potato Wedges, 60
   Spanish Potato and Onion Tapas, 229
   Stuffed New Potatoes, 227
   Twice-Baked Potatoes, 103
Presto-Pesto Bread, 160
Prosciutto
   Adriatic Antipasto, 139
   Chicken and Prosciutto Roulades, 78
   Chicken-Leek Filo Roll-Ups, 108
   Chicken-Prosciutto Meatballs, 236
   Parma Eggs, 47
   Neapolitan Slices, 162
Pumpkin
   Topsy-Turvy Maple-Walnut Pumpkin Muffins, 144

Radishes
   Stuffed Radish Roses, 63
Raisins
   Sicilian Stuffed Sole, 238
Ranch-Style Bean Dip, 212
Raspberry-Orange Turkey Kabobs, 237
Red currant jelly
   Red Wine Sauce, 84
Red Wine Sauce, 84
Rhineland Mini-Fajitas, 110
Rice
   Barbados Black Bean 'n' Rice Turkey Salad, 133
   Fruited Rice Salad, 131
   Orange Risotto with Turkey, 85
   Peppered Rice Salad with Goat Cheese, 132
   Risotto Pinwheel Wraps, 121
   Stuffed Grape Leaves, 117
   Thai Curried Turkey Wraps, 122
Rich Pastry, 174
Risotto Pinwheel Wraps, 121
Roast Pork and Apple Pizza, 154
Roquefort Torta, 97
Roquefort-Onion Rolls, 159
Rosy Eggs, 47

Salads, 123-141
Salami
   Deli Party Carousel, 35
   Deli-Potato Salad Wrap-Ups, 136
   Party French Wedges, 161
   Risotto Pinwheel Wraps, 121
Salmon Remoulade Dip, 192
Salmon-Stuffed Tomatoes, 66
Sampan Spread, 210
Sandwich fillings
   Chicken or Turkey Filling, 180
   Cream Cheese Filling, 181
   Egg Filling, 178
   Ham Filling, 182
   Sandwich Spreads, 176-177
   Tuna Filling, 179
Sandwich Spreads, 176-177
Sauces
   Dipping Sauce, 3, 111
   Fruit Salsa, 107

Index   245

Sauces (*cont.*)
   Grace's Salsa, 219
   Luau Sauce, 23
   Red Wine Sauce, 84
   Sour Cream Sauce, 233
   Sweet and Sour Sauce, 32
   Tahitian Dip, 6
   Tarragon-Butter Sauce, 2
Sauerkraut
   Mini-Reuben Rolls, 232
   Open-Face Mini-Reubens, 168
Sausage
   Alpine Cheese Frittata, 100
   Kaleidoscope Bean Toss, 134
   Layered Sausage and Mushroom Omelet, 99
   Sausage and Eggs with Tortilla Strips, 102
   Sausage-Stuffed Mushrooms, 58
   Smoked-Sausage Muffin Cups, 151
   Spanish Potato and Onion Tapas, 229
   Twice-Baked Potatoes, 103
Scallops
   Bouillabaisse-Style Seafood Bites, 12
   Curried Scallops and Fruit Kabobs, 19
Sesame-Crab Dumplings, 14
Sesame seeds, toasting, 109
Shangri-La Drumsticks, 75
Shiitake Pork Spring Rolls, 111
Shrimp
   Bouillabaisse-Style Seafood Bites, 12
   Butterflied Bayou Shrimp, 16
   Gingered Shrimp Balls, 18
   Grilled Ginger-Honey Shrimp, 91
   Mandarin Stir-Fry in Pita Bread, 169
   Pickled Shrimp, 17
   Shrimp and Black Bean Wraps, 118
   Treasure Island Shrimp, 239
Sicilian Stuffed Sole, 238
Skewered Szechuan-Style Barbecued Pork, 20
Small Meals, 71-104
Smoked Albacore Dip, 194
Smoked-Sausage Muffin Cups, 151
Smoky Cheese Log, 208
Smoky Deviled Eggs, 47
Soups
   Curried Sweet Potato Soup, 104
Sour cream
   Beefy-Mushroom Pinwheels, 34
   California Quiche, 98
   Caramelized Onion-Mustard Dip, 220
   Caviar-Crowned Mold, 209
   Confetti Polenta Cups, 40
   Green Goddess Dip, 206
   Roquefort Torta, 97
   Salmon Remoulade Dip, 192
   Sampan Spread, 210
   Sour Cream Sauce, 233
   Tahitian Dip, 6
   Zucchini Appetizer Pie, 68
South Seas Pork, 93
Spanish Potato and Onion Tapas, 229
Spiced Carrot Sticks, 55
Spicy Chops with Mango Glaze, 92
Spinach
   Risotto Pinwheel Wraps, 121
   Spinach-Filled Filo Cups, 64
Spring rolls
   Sweet-Hot Turkey Spring Rolls, 109
   Shiitake Pork Spring Rolls, 111

Squash
   Cheese-Stuffed Zucchini, 67
   Double-Squash Cups, 62
   Garden-Path Dip with Pita Wedges, 218
   Green 'n' Gold Vegetable Nachos, 226
   Zucchini Appetizer Pie, 68
   Zucchini Bites, 69
Stuffed Brussels Sprouts, 54
Stuffed Cucumber Slices, 56
Stuffed Edam Cheese, 207
Stuffed Grape Leaves, 117
Stuffed Mushrooms Supreme, 231
Stuffed New Potatoes, 227
Stuffed Radish Roses, 63
Stuffed Snow Peas, 59
Stuffed Turkey Roll-Ups with Red Wine Sauce, 84
Sun-dried tomatoes
   Chicken and Prosciutto Roulades, 78
   Eggplant Pâté, 228
   Giant Chicken-Stuffed Shells, 79
   Herb-Parmesan Muffins, 145
   Neapolitan Slices, 162
   Parma Eggs, 47
   Stuffed New Potatoes, 227
   Sun-Dried Tomato Pasta, 127
   Venetian Crowns, 50
   Stuffed Mushrooms Supreme, 231
Sunset Ham Balls, 27
Sweet 'n' Spicy Riblets, 234
Sweet potatoes
   Curried Sweet Potato Soup, 104
   Sweet Potato Pecan Bread, 148
Sweet-Hot Turkey Spring Rolls, 109

Tahitian Dip, 6
Tahitian Sunset Roll-Ups, 6
Tangerines
   Cashew Chicken Pitas, 171
Tarragon-Butter Sauce, 2
Taste-of-Italy Dip, 204
Taste-of-Thai Bowl, 125
Taste-of-the-Tropics Grilled Chicken Burritos, 107
Teriyaki Roll-Ups, 30
Teriyaki sauce
   Crunchy Meatballs, 33
   Grilled Ginger-Honey Shrimp, 91
Thai Curried Turkey Wraps, 122
Thin-Crust Pizza, 158
Toasted Almond and Brie Slices, 36
Tomatoes
   Barbados Black Bean 'n' Rice Turkey Salad, 133
   Chili con Queso, 202
   Eat-with-Your-Hands Italian Salad, 129
   Eggplant Caviar, 214
   Eggplant Dip, 215
   Fruit Salsa, 107
   Garden-Path Dip with Pita Wedges, 218
   Grace's Salsa, 219
   Green 'n' Gold Vegetable Nachos, 226
   Hearty Pasta Salad Bowl, 126
   Kaleidoscope Bean Toss, 134
   Pesto-Stuffed Cherry Tomatoes, 65
   Pinto Salsa, 213
   Salmon-Stuffed Tomatoes, 66
   Sun-Dried Tomato Pasta, 127
   Tomato-Zucchini Mousse, 141
Topsy-Turvy Maple-Walnut Pumpkin Muffins, 144

Tortillas
   Bean and Goat Cheese Quesadillas, 116
   Falafel Taco Wraps, 119
   Korean Omelet Wraps, 114
   Peppered Beef Rolls, 233
   Pesto-Style Chicken Fajitas, 106
   Rhineland Mini-Fajitas, 110
   Sausage and Eggs with Tortilla Strips, 102
   Shrimp and Black Bean Wraps, 118
   Taste-of-the-Tropics Grilled Chicken Burritos, 107
   Thai Curried Turkey Wraps, 122
   Tortilla-Cheese Stack, 96
   Turkey Tortilla Crisp, 87
Treasure Island Shrimp, 239
Turkey
   All-American Turkey Meatballs, 8
   Almond-Cherry Turkey Cutlets, 82
   Barbados Black Bean 'n' Rice Turkey Salad, 133
   Easy Barbecued Turkey Cubes, 9
   Hot Open-Face Turkey Sandwich, 163
   Orange and Cranberry Turkey Loaf, 83
   Orange Risotto with Turkey, 85
   Pinto Bean and Turkey Chili, 86
   Raspberry-Orange Turkey Kabobs, 237
   Stuffed Turkey Roll-Ups with Red Wine Sauce, 84
   Sweet-Hot Turkey Spring Rolls, 109
   Thai Curried Turkey Wraps, 122
   Turkey Brochettes, 10
   Turkey Pâté, 191
   Turkey Tortilla Crisp, 87
Twice-Baked Potatoes, 103

Vegetable and Cheese-Stuffed Pitas, 170
Vegetable-Stuffed Pita Rounds, 172
Velvety Chicken Liver Pâté, 188

Walnuts
   Topsy-Turvy Maple-Walnut Pumpkin Muffins, 144
Water chestnuts
   Barbecued Porkburgers with Fresh Papaya Relish, 184
   Cashew Chicken Pitas, 171
   Chicken and Water Chestnuts, 80
   Crab and Swiss on Sourdough, 183
   Crunchy Meatballs, 33
   Gingered Shrimp Balls, 18
   Hot Open-Face Turkey Sandwich, 163
   Mandarin Stir-Fry in Pita Bread, 169
   Meatballs with Luau Sauce, 23
   Pesto-Style Chicken Fajitas, 106
   Sesame-Crab Dumplings, 14
   Stuffed Turkey Roll-Ups with Red Wine Sauce, 84
   Sweet-Hot Turkey Spring Rolls, 109
   Teriyaki Roll-Ups, 30
   No-Liver Chutney Rumaki, 28
Wild West Salad, 135
Wonton wrappers
   Curried Pork Fold-overs, 112
   Italian Envelopes, 113

Yogacado Dip, 222

Zucchini Appetizer Pie, 68
Zucchini Bites, 69
Zucchini-Cheese Frittata, 101